THE DRUG TO CONTROL

HOW THE ELITE CONSPIRE AGAINST YOU

2

DECONSTRUCTING AMERICA PART 3

TOM S. PANE

FOREWORD

THIS book is the third part in a series entitled *Deconstructing America,* which attempts to explain, in a relatively easy-to-understand way, how the ultra-rich use their vast power and resources to manipulate the general population into supporting their beliefs and interests. The series will look at different aspects of how power is used to control people, all within the framework of the history and development of the United States of America, to illustrate its arguments and support its conclusions.

The first book in the series, *The Power to Control,* talks about how control is applied against the population by those in power through a variety of methods which include: the retelling of historical events in a narrative that aligns with the goals of the ultra-rich; the use of propaganda and the institutional framework of laws, courts and police to repress the majority in support of the wealthy elite minority; and an interconnected system of indoctrination programming and ongoing conditioning intended to help reinforce all of the above. The first book also discussed how elites use words and language, as well as the illusion of choice, to give American citizens the impression they live in a just and fair society.

The second book in the series, *The Money to Control,* focuses on how the ultra-rich use their own personal wealth, their influence with the government, and their ownership of industries and private property to not only repress and keep the lower classes unable to challenge their rule, but to steadily bleed the lower classes dry of their wealth through overwork and exploitation.

The third book in the series, *The Drug to Control,* examines the history of the global drug war, and how that once legal industry initially driven by colonialism and the exploitation of third-world nations became an underground black market, in which the very authorities who were vowing to stamp out the drug scourge simultaneously funded, armed, and provided transportation and protection to those very drug lords.

This book is the first in the series not to be based on Howard Zinn or Noam Chomsky's work. Instead, it is based on some of the most groundbreaking books on the drug war and international drug smuggling, which illuminate the US government's role in protecting and encouraging the global illicit drug racket.

The Drug to Control follows the legal and illicit drug trade and prohibition from its beginnings in the 16th century up to the 2000s through the following source material. I encourage readers who want to learn more to read these books in full. But worry not: the Deconstructing America series distills these books into an easy-to-consume format.

The Politics of Heroin in Southeast Asia

Acid Dreams: The Complete Social History of LSD: The CIA, The Sixties, and Beyond

Dark Alliance: The CIA, The Contras, and the Crack Cocaine Explosion

All of these books are expertly researched and are based on open public record sources; declassified US government documents; unclassified records released under the Freedom of Information Act (FOIA); congressional reports and hearing transcripts; transcripts and pleadings in state and federal courts; corporate records; and records from domestic and international law enforcement. All of the information, sans my witty commentary, is one hundred percent factual beyond reproach.

The Drug to Control, unlike the first two books, which are wholly focused on the United States, does look at the global situation, as drug smuggling and the drug war cannot be examined without looking at the international community in totality.

While reading the first two books is not required to understand this one, I would recommend you read them first (it only takes an hour or two) to set the playing field for this discussion.

One of the reasons I focus on historical events in these books, rather than present-day events, is that I feel it is critical to reset and reorient the conversation about what is happening in America by returning to the root incidents that led to the state we are in now. This is called the historical method for probing contemporary issues.

Until we can strip away decades of misinformation and disinformation that have obfuscated the facts about how drugs are used to pit one group against another, as well as weaken them to abuse and persecution by the state and the rich, no solution can be achieved, since the right conversations are simply not taking place.

The goal of this book is to allow you, the inhabitants of America, to live a freer and more authentic life by possessing alternate information that those in charge have decided not to provide to you.

INTRODUCTION

IF you read my first two books, you know I talk about how power and control are built and maintained through the manipulation of history as well as nuances in language and double meanings, which are all supported by highly sophisticated propaganda networks that manufacture a version of reality that is far detached from what it actually is. This narrative framework is meant to shape and illustrate our society to young people and the world at large, in line with the image it wants to portray – one that is positive, self-serving, and manufactured.

The Drug War, over the past century, has its own narrative framework and language that is intended to produce no significant understanding of the issues we all face or provide a path forward to attempt to resolve or mitigate the supposed personal and social issues from illicit drugs.

This inherent programmed and conditioned bias is part of the challenge. For example, in modern US society, an alcohol addict is an alcoholic who needs medical assistance and compassion, while anyone who is addicted to any illegal drug is a criminal and a social deviant who needs to be imprisoned and punished. There is no consistency in this logic.

When I started this book, I had no intention of focusing on covert intelligence operations and how they contributed to the drug war. What I found as I did my research and due diligence is that the story of the global drug war could not be told without understanding how, in the 20th century, illicit drug smuggling was intricately integrated with the clandestine military operations of countries like France, the US, and the UK, among many others.

After my research, I have concluded that the War on Drugs has nothing to do with public health or concern for the greater good or well-being of society as a whole. It is my argument that the Drug War is a mechanism for those in power to leverage control over their respective populations and captured colonial states, typically the poorer and darker-shaded ones, as well as inconvenient political opponents and dissidents that need to be vilified. It is also a great way to generate revenue for illegal, off-the-books military and intelligence operations.

But in the end, that is really only one way to use drugs to leverage power and implement control over individuals and groups for various benefits to the elite. Whether that power and control is about managing our own population or attempting to overthrow elected governments from other countries to install pro-US supporters into power forcibly, the drug war is in no way the entity that the American people think it is.

Historically, in the US, just like with other types of laws and regulations, drug laws and enforcement have been selectively applied to the most vulnerable groups who are ripe for exploitation. Traditionally targeted for selective repression include the poor, the underprivileged, racial minorities, leftists, and any dissenter of the state. Drug controls you will see time and time again are only enacted and enforced on these vulnerable groups during times of social crisis and upheaval, like when marijuana was outlawed in the black ghettos during the Depression with the Marijuana Tax Act of 1937. Or when LSD was illegalized in the 1960s as a response to the anti-war movement. See, these people are just whacked out on drugs; their issues with the war are not rational. Get it? Vilifying and criminalizing your political opponents and social issues gives the authorities carte blanche to attack and imprison those groups and people for non-dissidence-related reasons.

This book will examine the history of illegal drugs, and how they went from being legal and benign to one of the supposed great evils of the 20ᵗʰ-21ˢᵗ century. We will start by looking at the history of opium and colonialism, in which we can find the seeds of the modern drug trade. Then we will look at how drug prohibition first came about, and how it helped to create a massive network of criminal and enforcement gangs that would be intricately intertwined with the global economy and clandestine operations for the major Western and Eastern powers.

We will then look at how the CIA used illicit drugs to experiment on unknowing US citizens, which led to the leaking of LSD and psychedelics across the American youth population of the 1960s. We will then move on to the Nixon War on Drugs, which targeted leftist dissidents and black militants, to the Contra scandal of the 1980s, where the CIA shipped planeloads of cocaine into LA ghettos to fuel the so-called crack epidemic. Finally, we will wrap things up by seeing where the drug war went in the 1990s and early 2000s.

The global drug war is a complex, multi-headed beast, not easy to wrap one's mind around, since so much has been obfuscated in terms of propaganda, social programming, and conditioning. This book is intended to present the drug war in a way very different from the framework and narrative you have been spoon-fed throughout your life. It is backed by some of the best research and investigative journalism ever done in the US.

This book, like the rest of the Deconstructing America series, will show you the true America, without the fluff, the PR, the sappy stories, and the forbidden words and ideas that are not permitted to exist within the broader scope of American society.

Contents

PART 1: THE BEGINNING AND EVOLUTION OF THE DRUG WAR

THE history of what are now illegal drugs is a modern phenomenon, only existing in the last few hundred years, when drugs like opium were eventually illegalized after nation-states and corporations had forcibly polluted the world's populations with opioid addiction for profit, wealth, power, and control.

THE REAL HISTORY OF OPIUM

OPIUM is an extract from the poppy plant and has been cultivated and traded across all of Asia for over a thousand years, mainly in a medicinal capacity. Opium is mentioned in ancient Assyrian, Egyptian, Greek, and Roman pharmacological records dating back to the Bronze Age. Its origins trace back to the eastern Mediterranean and were traded as far away as China in the 8th century AD. Opium's use as a folk and formal medicine dates back well over 5,000 years.

Eventually, opium production and transportation would be centralized across about 5,000 miles of mountainous terrain in Southeast Asia, eventually being called *The Golden Triangle*. By 1996, 96% of the world's illicit opium growing was found in this zone. It will be later in the book that you'll find out how that happened.

Opium and other popular drugs like the coca leaf (synthesized into cocaine) were used medicinally for thousands of years, somehow without destroying the fabric of society. The reality of the legacy of the drug war is that it was modern businesses and modern corporations that created the 20th-century illegal drug market, along with manufacturing millions and millions of drug addicts. Just like heroin and cocaine were creations of the modern pharmaceutical industry, today's popular synthetic stimulants were also developed by the same companies (Merck, J&J, Bayer, and others). Amphetamines were first synthesized in 1887, MDMA in 1914, and methamphetamine in 1919. None of these drugs are new, just the propaganda surrounding them. But what really laid the foundation for the modern drug trade is opium. The eventual prohibition of opium is what created the enforcement agencies and criminal networks whose interactions helped shape the rest of the illicit drug market for centuries to come.

It was not until the 16th century that people in Persia and India began eating and drinking opium mixtures as a pleasurable pastime, not medicine. Dutch merchants witnessed Chinese people smoking an opium-tobacco mixture in Indonesia in 1617. And it was these civilized European business merchants who discovered opium's commercial potential in the 17th century, regardless of the human and social damage it caused. During this time, European shipments of smoking opium between India and China created one of the world's most lucrative trade triangles, *the Golden Triangle.*

Opium was quite the business opportunity for the Dutch, as profits from the opium trade were sky-high. They were able to buy opium cheaply in India and sell it in Java for a **400% profit margin** by 1679. By 1681, opium accounted for 34% of all cargo on Asian ships sailing out of Jakarta. Not a bad business model.

While Portuguese merchants were the first to ship cargoes of opium from India to China, it was the Dutch who made the shipping of opium a large-scale commercial venture. It was also the Dutch who introduced the practice of smoking opium in a pipe, helping to popularize opium use among the Chinese population. As the Chinese population saw opium addiction and abuse devastate their society, the Chinese emperor instituted the first failed opium ban in 1729.

For three centuries, the Dutch created the largest and most lucrative of the colonial opium monopolies. By 1929, it was still operating 1,065 opium dens that retailed 59 tons of opium to 101,000 registered smokers in their captured colonies.

In the late 18th century, the opium trade accelerated, for under the doctrines of mercantilism, all the major world powers used the commercialization of drugs (opium, caffeine, nicotine) in their colonial ventures to generate profit and wealth, leading to more power and control over their own populations and their colonies. For instance, the Dutch controlled Java's coffee exports, the Spanish controlled a tobacco monopoly in the Philippines, and the British controlled the Bengal opium trade.

It was the Europeans, in their quest for power, control, and wealth, who were responsible for transforming all these drugs from medicinal or luxury goods into commodities of mass consumption, integrating them into the lifestyles and economies of economies across the world. And it is not a coincidence that the modern drug era coincides with Europe's so-called *Age of Discovery*.

These colonial powers, through force and violence, divvied up the rest of the world (non-advanced military powers) and made them open up their economies and societies to force the opium trade from their colonizers. It was the Western power empire builders who subjected and addicted millions of natives to opium addiction, generating obscene revenue for more colonial expansion (military ventures) and more profit for the elite ruling classes.

THE true modern era of opium began in 1773, when the British East India Company (BEIC), which at the time was the colonial ruler of Bengal in northern India, imposed a monopoly over the production and sale of opium. For 130 years, Britain actively promoted the export of Indian opium to China, in violation of the national Chinese anti-drug laws. Through this monopoly, the BEIC increased opium production from 75 tons in 1776 to 3,200 tons in 1850.

Now, the Chinese didn't much like the British infecting their entire population with a disease for profit, understandably so, so the Chinese made it illegal in the 1790s, but that didn't stop the British.

In all their empathy and glory, the British Empire launched two Opium Wars (1839, 1858) against the Chinese to force them to rescind their opium ban, at the end of a gun.

When the Chinese tried to confiscate opium coming into their country by British merchants and smugglers, the British sent a fleet of ships and thousands of troops and captured Canton in 1839, and then spent the next two years looting and sacking Chinese coastal sites until the Chinese were forced to sue for peace. For this, China gave the British Hong Kong (huh, no wonder they wanted it back?), had to open five ports to opium smugglers, and paid $21 million to the British for destroying their opium shipments. How does this sound for law and order to you?

Then, during the 2nd opium War, the British and French ganged up on the Chinese and forced them to open their country to free European trade. The British won this one too, and forced the Chinese to have unrestricted growth in both imports and addicts. I can't imagine why the East does not trust Western powers.

See, no black-market, slimy drug dealers here—just respectable countries and companies using and abusing native populations and resources for their own benefit. By 1900, China's population of 400 million people had 13.5 million opium addicts who consumed 38,000 tons of opium annually. By 1906, 27% of all adult Chinese males were opium smokers. Nice work, UK and the royal family! How do you like those pictures of Prince George, everyone?

It was during the 19th century that the British entirely transformed opium from a luxury good for the few to a bulk-traded commodity for the masses, like coffee and tea. In the late 19th century, opium use spread beyond China and into Southeast Asia and Europe. In fact, ALL the European colonial governments in Southeast Asia generated tax revenues by selling opium to locals through state-owned opium dens. Opium was so crucial to the British Empire that during the 19th century, it was responsible for 6% to 15% of British India's tax revenues.

By the time Britain finally abandoned its advocacy of the international drug trade in 1907, opium had become a global commodity very similar to coffee, cocoa, tea, or tobacco. All thanks to countries like Britain, the Netherlands, France, the US, and the like. You know, the civilized nations.

France is a vital colonizer to mention since it was their abandoned colonial war that brought the US to Vietnam in the 1950s – 1970s, which further helped to expand and solidify the international drug market.

In 1858, a French invasion fleet arrived off the coast of Vietnam at Saigon, established a garrison, and occupied much of the Mekong Delta. The Vietnamese were not able to eject the French invaders from their land, so they were forced to give the French three provinces around Saigon and pay an indemnity worth 4 million francs. The French saw the profit potential from opium in Saigon. As they invaded and colonized other countries, like Cambodia in 1863, Annam in 1883, Tonkin in 1884, and Laos in 1893, they imposed opium monopolies in every country they illegally annexed. By 1918, French Indochina was home to 1,512 opium dens and 3,098 retail shops. At the beginning of WW2, the French imported almost 60 tons of opium annually from Iran and Turkey to supply 100,000 addicts in French Indochina.

Is it possible that this history of the French forcing opium on the populations of Southeast Asia could have aided in the growth and development of Communism in the area? Communists used to identify addicts and send them to drug clinics where opium use was denounced as an "imperialist and capitalist activity." Some of Ho Chi Minh's most effective propaganda targeted French officials who ran the state opium monopoly. With an addiction rate of 20% of the entire population, it was a significant issue that helped lead to the rejection of Western values, capitalism, and colonialism.

It is an undeniable fact that the global opium market and trade were a direct result of European colonialism, and would not have existed or developed as it did without it.

IN 1805, morphine, the active narcotic in opium, was first extracted by pharmaceutical companies, beginning the age of pharmaceutical drugs. Merck began commercial manufacturing morphine in 1827, but it did not become popular as an anesthetic until the 1860s, when injection by syringe was made possible. In 1874, a researcher invented diacetylmorphine by boiling morphine and acetic anhydride over a stove. This researcher, based on his observations, believed there was no medicinal value in his invention, so he stopped working with it after seeing the horrible effect it had on dog test subjects. But lucky for us, Bayer was not limited by such moral concerns. In 1898, Bayer, you know them, right? The friendly aspirin people. Well, they began mass-producing diacetylmorphine and named it **HEROIN**. In their global marketing campaign, with zero supporting scientific evidence, Bayer promoted heroin as a nonaddictive cure for adult ailments like coughing and infant respiratory diseases. Who wouldn't want their baby to be on heroin? It gets better.

In 1906, the American Medical Association (AMA) approved heroin for general use "in place of morphine in various painful injections." Contrary to all the evidence about the addition of opiates, of which there was a significant amount, doctors and physicians, without scientific proof, promoted heroin as an effective, **nonaddictive** substitute for morphine and opium. Heroin is nonaddictive? Hysterical! So, if respectable scientists and doctors weren't filling people's heads with such lies and nonsense, would people have been so trusting of these drugs overall? Reminds me very much of the modern opioid cruises driven by the Sackler family. OxyContin was promoted by doctors, with zero scientific evidence, as less addictive than other narcotics. Similar results followed.

It was also during the 19th century that Europeans became aware of the coca leaf, which Andean Indians had used for medicinal and stimulant purposes for over 8,000 years. And yet again, it is the colonial pharmaceutical companies that turned this medicinal folk medicine into a horror, as in the 1850s, Merck began to manufacture crystalline cocaine. Yet again, with zero supporting scientific evidence or data, doctors and scientists were amazed by cocaine and promoted all its outstanding qualities. Regular food and drink companies started infusing cocaine into their products, the most famous being Coca-Cola. Pharmaceutical companies produced lines of cocaine cigarettes, hypodermic capsules, ointments, and sprays.

The mass marketing of cocaine and heroin is what created mass addiction across the global population.

Not slimy drug pushers, not the mafia, but regular, everyday corporations without regulation, exploiting people's health and wellbeing for profit, all while misleading people about the dangers of such substances. The stooge doctor and scientist class was instrumental in normalizing addictive drug use as a way to manage personal health issues. They did this without any evidence to support their claims. This should make you wonder about what doctors and scientists are really doing if not promoting dangerous substances as a way to make money for their corporations and handlers.

All of this, not coincidentally, happened at the same time as industrialization was moving workers around the world from agrarian farmers to factory workers. Well, now that the needs of industry and machines were driving people, the factory worker was doped up on stimulants to keep them going through their brutal 12-hour hour/7-day-a-week wage-slave work schedule. In addition to the more exotic stimulants like cocaine, to adjust to working in the new industrialized world, people's consumption of sugar and caffeine jumped 3 to 4 times what it was prior. We are still dealing with these changes today in terms of individual and public health.

And if the American workers needed to be jacked up all day on stimulants like caffeine and sugar to keep them going, they needed something to come down at night for the brief few hours they had to rest. The solution was legal over-the-counter 'medicines' that had morphine and heroin in them to help you come down. Doctors were all too happy to advocate for opium, shooting women up with morphine to calm their nerves, and doping up babies and children with opium and heroin tonics.

"Opium was the Victorians' aspirin, Valium, and Nyquil, which could be bought at the local chemist for as little as a penny." - Historian Terry Parssinen.

Huh, I wonder why that cheap drug is so expensive now? This book explains why in detail. Stick around.

Then came the early 20th century, and once the sophisticated enlightened powers saw the horrific toll drugs were taking on their own upper-crust citizens, keeping in mind they couldn't have cared less when it was the Chinese who were being destroyed, they decided to punish their own people for the horrors the ruling class oligarchy and their corporate stooges foist on them with draconian anti-drug laws. But it was to be for naught, as the merchants and elite royalty and their corporations ensured opium and illegal drugs were now so ingrained into culture and society that they could not be eradicated with such tactics.

THE main thing that stopped all those miracle tonic solutions infused with highly addictive drugs was when the 1906 U.S. Pure Food and Drug Act required that patent medicines display their contents on the bottle or package. Sales of these remedies immediately dropped by one-third. It seems that all you have to do is let consumers know what they are buying without deceit, and they are smart enough not to want to give their kids heroin to help them with the sniffles. How can consumers have this much common sense when doctors do not? This is a good question, and this type of elitist mind control is a lot of what my books are all about: how people are manipulated to serve the interests of the super-rich, usually at their own expense.

It turns out, contrary to common belief, that the more educated you are and integrated into the elitist system, the more programmed and conditioned you are. This is counterintuitive to most people, who think smart people are less susceptible to manipulation. This is a fallacy. Brilliant people are among the most malleable to manipulation and coercion. Their egos and narcissism may have something to do with it. All intelligent people out there with such high opinions of yourselves are going to have a hard time accepting this truism.

Also, in 1906, the British Parliament passed a motion to end the Indian/China opium trade, which it had run. But too late for China, which already had its general population heavily addicted to opium and heroin thanks to the British, and could not easily wipe them out.

Prohibition was driven in part by religious fundamentalists who were now very offended and horrified that drugs like opium and heroin were being used and abused by upper-class white Christians in first-world countries. This was not an issue for them for hundreds of years, while the non-Christian, savage heathens of their colonial empires were deliberately addicted and forced to accept the colonial oppressor pushing drugs on their populations, sometimes at the end of a gun.

"This opium trade is a Christian monopoly. Its history is a Christian sin, a Christian shame." - Rev. A. E. Moule, Shanghai Missionary Conference, 1877

The global narcotics prohibition movement started in the 1870s. The modern drug war and all issues related to the criminalization of what are now illicit drugs began at this time in the modern era. Before this time, never in human history have drugs and what a human being consumes in their body been regulated in such a fashion. This criminalization of the drug trade and drug users created a system and framework of repression, where governments and individuals would leverage drug money as a tool to gain power and control over their respective populations. While the cover story for drug illegalization is about public and individual health and social well-being, the evidence is to the contrary.

The criminalization of drugs has led to more abuse, more crime, more social destabilization, and more negative social effects than before criminalization. And when I say before criminalization, I mean before colonial powers and their merchants and Christian missionaries made addictive drugs a legal and encouraged habit and activity by native populations.

They created it, and now they don't like what they made, so they want to punish you for their crimes and mistakes. This is precisely how the ultra-rich operate.

Look at the current opioid crisis, which was led and driven by the Sackler family, people who have not seen any level of accountability for their key roles in creating and perpetuating the modern opioid crisis. The result of this is millions of Americans addicted to OxyContin, and now pharmaceutical companies and the DEA are limiting medications people need for actual surgeries as an excuse to fight the opioid epidemic. The ultra-rich create these horrific situations by exploiting the citizenry and then blaming the very people they abused and exploited. This process goes on to this very day.

The USA's role in the global drug prohibition really started with its purchase of the Philippines from Spain in 1899. After it purchased the Philippines, along with 7,000 islands and six million Filipinos (nice that people can be bought like that as a whole country), and a state opium monopoly that sold at the time 130 tons of opium through 190 licensed opium dens. Five years later, the US outlawed all opium smoking in the Philippines. This critical event begins the USA's century-plus-long, emotion-driven, unhinged campaign of global drug prohibition and enforcement.

In 1909, the US Congress passed the Smoking Opium Exclusion Act, which banned imports of smoking opium. At the Hague two years later, the International Opium Convention of 1912 restricted all nonmedical use of opium. To further this new anti-drug positioning, the US enacted the Harrison Narcotics Act of 1914, which was essentially the beginning of the official drug war in the USA, requiring a doctor's prescription to buy narcotics legally. In 1919, furthering this trend of individual repression and intolerance, the US passed the Volstead Act, which prohibited alcohol sales. In 1923, to enforce all these new laws, the Narcotics Division was created, the first US drug enforcement agency. Good times!

How did this all go? Well, you know, a century-plus later, it was, and continues to be an unmitigated failure in every way.

The prohibition of drugs and alcohol led the whole commercial market to move underground and be taken over by organized crime. Illegalization created a vast illicit economy, as the legal drug economy had to go somewhere, so it went dark.

The decline in legal drugs and sales did not stop or reduce addiction in the USA, far from it. Now, people went to illegal drug dealers instead of doctors or pharmacists, allowing organized crime to expand from more local gangs to national syndicates who could use their capital to buy police and political payoffs for access to power. Although Americans dummied up and legalized alcohol again in 1933, reducing income and power to criminal gangs, drug and narcotic prohibition stayed in place, giving organized crime a nice wealth foundation to build up their organizations post-WW2.

After the establishment of prohibition in the 1920s, narcotics like opium and heroin were shifted from legal commerce, in which corporations pushed their addictive drugs on citizens while lying about their harm and addictive qualities, to illicit commerce that would grow in the post-WW2 world economy to help fund government clandestine activities, criminal gangs, warlords, terrorists, and other covert operations.

All the legislation supposedly intended to mitigate or eradicate the drug trade and drug usage has had the opposite effect, year after year. Drug policies have been counterproductive, self-defeating, and ineffective, leading to more negative drug-related personal, medical, and social issues than ever existed before prohibition.

The cold, hard reality of it is that governments never really tried in earnest to mitigate drug addiction and the drug trade. They undermined their own policies from day one since they were using illegal drugs to fund all sorts of things that one cannot use legal money for, like covert operations of intelligence services, of which lots will be discussed in this book.

In fact, the government took on a protectionist stance on drug smugglers they aligned with on political issues, and a prohibitive stance on drug smugglers that did not align with the political and nationalist goals. In this, countries, from the earliest days of drug prohibition, played both sides of the field, both prosecuting and persecuting minor drug users and taking down big, famous drug lords only AFTER they had fallen from grace and were no longer a significant force in the trade. This has resulted in decades of big PR busts of huge ex-drug lords, lots of harassment of low-level drug users, and little to no actual impact on drug manufacturing, smuggling, or addiction.

It's essential to recognize that many of the drug trade issues were in lockstep with the broader issues of power and control, aligned to the supposed *Cold War* between the USSR and the USA. The leaders of the USA thought it was justified to employ any method needed to stop the horrors of Communism, something made possible by the massive propaganda infrastructure to which US leaders are exposed.

THE Cold War is intricately linked to the growth and development of the illicit drug supply chain and market. It was the rationale of containment and the any-means-to-an-end mentality to fight Communism that drove the Western powers, like the USA, to use illegal drugs as a way to undermine Communist rule, as well as fund clandestine activities intended to bring down or impact Communist states and leftist movements. In this, the drug war is a tool, although how effective it is questionable, to be used as leverage in a tug-of-war for power and control with the then-Soviet bloc.

Now, one could pontificate that the horrific tolls imposed on Far Eastern peoples by the British and other colonial powers in forcing opium addiction on them for profit and power created the very conditions required for a people's revolution. One of the first things the Communist Party did was to get opium under control in China, so it's not hard to connect these two situations and see cause and effect.

After the successful Chinese Communist Revolution of 1949, the Communist Party launched an anti-opium campaign that included mass mobilization and compulsory treatment. Through this, China was able to convert its population of opium addicts to being mostly drug-free by the mid-1950s. Chinese communists eventually extended their influence to the rest of Southeast Asia to further reduce opium manufacturing and smuggling.

As for the USA, while on the international stage, it was acting very moral and anti-drug, it was in fact protecting major international drug traffickers through US covert operations, all in the name of fighting the most horrible thing in the world, according to American leaders - Communism.

To lead this mighty ideological battle for our souls, in 1947, the US created the Central Intelligence Agency (CIA), a department supposedly for international espionage and covert operations. As you will find out in the pages of this book, from the CIA's own memos, the CIA, from day one, was operating in an illegal and criminal capacity on American soil. It was the CIA that really embraced drugs as a method for power and control, both over its own citizens and other nationalities. CIA agents quickly made alliances with international drug smugglers and far-right police state goons looking for allies in their eternal battle against the evils of Communism and workers' rights.

While this new international focus on drug prohibition did manage to reduce the legal opium trade and usage overall, people moved over to the latest, supposedly non-addictive alternatives to opium, like heroin, made by pharmaceutical companies like Bayer and Merck.

While national propaganda told citizens and the world at large how horrible these drugs were, at the same time, those very countries' intelligence agencies and governments were supporting, funding, arming, and protecting, as mafioso enforcers, the same drug lords and criminal gangs we said were the scourge of the world. The US government, and others, played both sides of the drug war from the earliest days, both acting as global prohibition officers, as well as enforcers and protectors of larger drug syndicates and traffickers, at least the ones that were in alignment with US political and corporate objectives of the ruling elite.

If this combination of both prohibition and protection sounds a lot like a mafia protection racket, you would be correct. There is no difference.

It was US covert operations being run in the name of containment policy in Washington that did the most to build up a centralized, large-scale commercial framework of illegal drug smuggling post-WW2.

The first major operation in this process was a CIA covert op in Burma in the 1950s, supporting the exiled Chinese Nationalist party (KMT), once the Communists took over China, allowing the KMT to become massive drug smugglers and kingpins. The second major CIA operation in this vein was in Laos in the 1960s, where CIA planes were used to smuggle opium around the *Golden Triangle*. To continue this was Afghanistan in the 1980s, as well as Central America and the Contras, as the CIA looked to prop up and arm any group it deemed a good ally in the grand ideological fight against the horrors of workers' rights. During these covert operations, the CIA mobilized tribal armies and gave them arms, money, transport aircraft, and protection, allowing them to become global drug lords.

It turns out, the interests and goals of the US elite and their stooges are right in line with international drug kingpins and mafiosos. The close relationship between the mafia and the US government will be made clear in these pages and is central to the power and control of the US general population in the 20th century.

Oh, there are lots and lots of more people, organizations, and countries with their hands in the till than just US intelligence. For these large-scale international drug operations to function, they need not just political and military protection and air transport, but banking services and financial support from countries like Taiwan and Pakistan.

BEGINNING right after WW2, US diplomats and the CIA assisted and supported illegal drug trafficking in three main ways. First, through alliances with major drug traffickers to help fund covert operations. Second, by protecting and concealing their criminal buddies from investigation. And third, by being actively involved in the transport of drugs (e.g., using CIA-owned Air America planes to ship them).

The US intelligence services have a long history of partnership and alliance with the mafia. In Sicily, Italy, the Office of Strategic Services (OSS), the forerunner to the CIA, allied with the Italian Mafia to help the Allied forces with their invasion of Italy in 1943. In Marseille, the CIA teamed up with the Corsican gangster underworld to revive and build up illegal international drug trafficking by ending workers' dock strikes in 1947 and 1950 that threatened funding for the Marshall Plan and the First Indochina War.

It was the prohibition of alcohol in 1920 that really sent the gangsters into the stratosphere, making household names of Al Capone, Bugsy Siegel, Dutch Schultz, and Meyer Lansky. One of the leading characters in the establishment of the American mafia was Lucky Luciano, who allied the Italian Mafia and Meyer Lansky's Jewish gangs for almost 40 years. When alcohol prohibition was about to end a few years later, the mob needed to move their business operations and funding somewhere else, and heroin was the perfect replacement.

This aligned well with Luciano's other major modernized operation, prostitution at scale. Luciano discovered that if you addict your prostitutes to heroin, they would be easier to manage and control, and could only support their expensive habit through further prostitution. This has been the standard method for control of pimps since the 1930s to keep prostitutes domiciled and obedient. See, everything comes back to power and control, which is what these books are all about.

Through the 1920s in Italy, the mafia was on the run thanks to dictator Benito Mussolini and his black-shirt fascist street thugs, who did not want to share power with the traditional mafioso. This led many mafia members to relocate to places like the USA, where, during WW2, they were actually very welcome. With the US government concerned about sabotage at its docks during WW2, it partnered with the mafia to protect shipping. Through this partnership, the US government worked directly with Luciano, who was gathering intelligence for the US for its invasion of Sicily.

After the Allies invaded Italy, the US military partnered with the mafia during the occupation phase, preferring to put mafiosos in power over the defeated fascist loyalists. This helped to reestablish the mafia's foothold in Italy after Mussolini had all but eliminated them from power.

While this was happening, Nazi resistance movements were gaining steam in Italy and France, which the US did not like very much. How strange. I thought the US was really anti-fascist and hated the Nazis so much. Well, it seems the US was not as liberal as it claims, as it did not like or support any Nazi resistance group that espoused fair and equitable treatment for all workers and citizens. Aka, they were too Communist.

In response, the US began to cut back its arms drops to the resistance in mid-1944. Thanks for the help, guys, now go F yourselves! This fear of anything left of center led the allies to appoint mafioso leaders to the new Italian interim government as a way of staving off any potential communist or leftist gains. In fact, when the US Army liberated Naples in 1943, the Italian military government hired New York gangster and racketeer

Vito Genovese as "interpreter for the Allied Military Government in Italy." Wow, how is that for cozy?

Then, in 1946, Lucky Luciano was released from prison and deported to Italy, allowing him to reestablish his mafia leadership and rebuild the international heroin trade post-war. The minute Luciano arrived in Italy, he started building an international narcotic syndicate that would last for decades. For more than a decade, this syndicate moved morphine base from the Middle East to Europe, transformed it into heroin, and then exported it to the US, without a single significant arrest or drug seizure. Hmm, they must have had some protection from up high, like the CIA. With Luciano's new narcotics network, they increased the number of US heroin addicts from 20,000 at the end of WW2 to 60,000 in 1952 and to 150,000 by 1965.

Luciano's operation wasn't just protected by military intelligence but by all levels within certain governments. For instance, the directors of Beirut Airport, Lebanese customs, and Lebanese narcotics police, along with the chief of police, all protected the import of raw opium from Turkey into Lebanon, its processing into morphine base, and its export to the labs in Sicily and Marseille.

In the end, it was Marseille, France, that would become the world's heroin laboratory for the next few decades, and it was the CIA's alliance with Corsican mafia syndicates that allowed that to happen. The gangsters allied with fascists to attack Communist demonstrators in the 1930s, worked with the Nazis to spy on the Communist underground in WW2, and got paid by the CIA to break Communist strikes in 1947 and 1950. From 1948 to 1972, the Corsican mafia controlled the US heroin market, in alliance with the US mafia for distribution, supplying about 80 percent of the USA's heroin supply. All done with the blessing and protection of the CIA.

Just like in the USA after every major war, in France, post-WW2 blue-collar workers were not seeing the benefits of post-war recovery like the rich were. Workers were putting in long hours, and saw improved production and output, all while being paid subsistence slave wages. In fact, prodded by their American economic advisors, who wielded tremendous power after the war, the French government deliberately kept worker wages low.

By 1947, while industrial production had been restored to pre-war levels, the average wage in France was 65% lower than during the Depression.

So, post-war workers were making less than they did during the depression? During this time, food prices had skyrocketed, and the average worker was eating 18 percent less than in 1938. The elite literally starve their own people when their personal profit is at stake. At this time in France, as in the USA now, the tax burden was entirely on the working and lower classes. It was so inequitable that the French publication Le Monde called it "more iniquitous than that which provoked the French Revolution."

Are these words ringing a bell for you, US citizens of today? Why are you working full-time or even 2-3 jobs, and can't afford the necessities, while the USAs and world elite get richer with their 8th mega yacht and 4th major league sports team purchase? Wars, just like other times of social disruption and upheaval, are opportunistic events for the ruling elite to exploit and rob the lower classes of work and wealth through exploitation.

IT turns out, based on congressional testimony and government records, that the CIA had a really tight and collaborative relationship with international mafia syndicates to achieve their goals and objectives, which, not coincidentally, are very similar. One CIA operative called both groups' practitioners of "the clandestine arts", meaning both groups operate outside the normal channels of civil society. (Aka criminals).

In pursuit of its political objectives, the CIA partners closely at different times with Sicilian and Corsican gangsters, Nationalist Chinese exiles, Lao generals, Afghan warlords, Haitian colonels, Panamanian generals (Noriega), Honduran smugglers, and Nicaraguan Contras.

At different times and in differing capacities, tribal warlords were supplied with and used CIA weapons, supplies, logistics, and political protection, allowing them to become major drug kingpins, expanding local opium production in their areas and exporting heroin to international markets where it was more profitable. The CIA made no effort to impede this drug trafficking. As proven in the 80s, they actually encouraged and supported it directly, while blocking investigations by the DEA and other agencies into their and their partners' criminal activities. This created drug-free trade zones in any of the areas where CIA covert ops were in process, where drug lords had full reign to conduct business in enforcement-free zones, in places like Panama, Afghanistan, and Laos.

Once the CIA secret war ended and they moved on to other objectives in different countries, the drug lords were left in place with all those arms and infrastructure to continue to build an international drug cartel for decades. From the CIA's POV, this was not their problem; their objective was met, time to move on. All of this is not conjecture but proven fact, based on CIA and government documentation.

After the CIA intervened in Burma by supporting the exiled Nationalist Chinese Party (KMT) in the 1950s, Burma's opium production rose from 18 tons in 1958 to 600 tons in 1970. During the CIA's covert war in Afghanistan in the 1980s (remember that one, where we supported Saddam Hussein?), Afghanistan's opium harvest increased from an estimated 100 tons in 1971 to 2,000 tons in 1991, rising to 4,600 tons following the war. Not surprisingly, in the decades following covert operations, Afghanistan, Burma, and Laos became the world's leading opium producers.

From 1948 to 1950, the CIA partnered with the Corsican gangster underworld to fight the French Communist Party for control over the strategic Mediterranean port of Marseille. With funding, supplies, and arms from the CIA, the Corsicans won control of the Marseille waterfront and then used it to become one of the top exporters of heroin to the US market for decades.

Around the same time, in Southeast Asia, the CIA ran a variety of covert operations on the Chinese border supporting the exiled Chinese Nationalist Party, which in turn led to the creation of the *Golden Triangle* heroin trading and smuggling system for decades. In 1950, the CIA armed those remnants of the Nationalist Chinese Army for an invasion of southwestern China, which never happened. Over the next decade, the Chinese Nationalist forces transformed the northern part of Burma into the world's largest opium producer, all under the funding and protection of the CIA.

The CIA also supplied and armed the Taiwanese government, police, and army through its front organization, a cutout called

Sea Supply Organization, which was in fact *Air America*. The CIA used *Air America* planes to send naval boats, arms, armed vehicles, and aircraft to the Taiwanese police force, building them up into an anti-Communist support system. But the guy running Taiwan, General Phao, was incredibly corrupt, and he used the CIA funding and arms to take over vice rackets like prostitution, drug smuggling, and protection schemes. The NYT called this man a "superlative crook," whom other Thai diplomats described as the "worst man in the history of Thailand." Nice partner for the CIA, huh? By 1955, Phao's national police force had become the largest opium trafficking syndicate in Thailand, all thanks to the funding and support of the CIA. Under General Phao's leadership and the CIA's support, Taiwan became the world's most crucial opium distribution center.

By the end of the 1950s, Burma, Laos, and Thailand had become home to more than half the world's opium supply. And in 1955, when the French got their asses kicked by the native population of Vietnam, that was when the US came in and took over the French operations lock, stock, and barrel, including their illegal opium smuggling operation called *Operation X*, which the CIA picked up to fund clandestine operations. During this period, the US broke the Geneva peace agreement made between the French and Vietnamese, as well as international law. We created the nation of South Vietnam to fight Communist interests in the area, supposedly.

Then, in the late 1970s, claiming to need to counter the Soviet invasion of Afghanistan, the CIA and the Pakistan Inter-Service Intelligence provided support and backing to Afghan warlords who used the CIA's logistics, arms, supplies, and funding to become some of the world's biggest drug lords.

It seems the USA is okay with making friends with big drug lords when they serve their purposes.

This cozy relationship among the mob, the CIA, and other wealthy individuals can be traced back to institutions such as Castle Bank and Trust. This bank was a shady money repository in the Bahamas that catered to mobsters, entertainers, drug dealers, and Republican party elitists. Richard Nixon deposited his cash there, and so did Tony Curtis, Creedence Clearwater Revival, Hugh Hefner, and Howard Hughes.

But Castle Bank was no ordinary bank. The CIA set it up as a cutout for supplying funding for a wide range of covert operations and as a money wash for a worldwide financial network managed by US intelligence. The CIA used Castle to facilitate the hidden transfer of large sums of money to finance subversion, paramilitary operations, coup d'états, bribery, and payments to foreign informants. Castle Bank played a key role in funding the CIA's secret war against Cuba, a campaign that employed mafia hit teams to work with the CIA to assassinate Fidel Castro.

IT turns out the CIA will partner with literally ANYONE, as long as it aligns with their current policy objectives, and in 1947, that was anyone who was against the Communists was an ally of the CIA. This includes gangsters, drug dealers, socialists, or ex-Nazi Gestapo officers.

Post-WW2 is an essential time for the modern international drug trade, as its infrastructure and relationships were defined by the USA's position against workers' rights and Communism. In response to anti-Communist sentiments, President Harry Truman established the Marshall Plan and the CIA with $400 million in funding. This money and the CIA were to be "used overtly in Greece and Turkey and covertly in France and Italy, through the CIA, to support.... democratic political parties." (aka pro-US business parties)

At the beginning of the Cold War, the CIA determined that unions would be key in their fight against Communism and workers' rights. You heard that right, too. Unions are anti-worker. Working through the American Federation of Labor (AFL), which was already operating a secret network in Europe to undermine workers' rights, the CIA began sending $2 million per year to anti-Communist labor leaders.

In 1947, the CIA, through its partnership with the Socialist Party in France, sent agents and a psychological warfare team to Marseille. The CIA supplied arms and money to Corsican gangs for assaults on communist picket lines and harassment of important union officials. The gangsters whom the CIA supported murdered several striking workers and assaulted and beat picketers. The CIA's psychological warfare team prepared and distributed pamphlets, broadcasts, and posters with the intent of discouraging workers from striking.

These tactics were very successful and have been ever since. On Dec. 9, Marseilles workers abandoned the strike, and this broke the strikes across the rest of France as well. Through this op, the CIA was instrumental in restoring Corsican gangsters' power structure and control over Marseille, leading to their further control over heroin manufacturing and distribution.

By the early 1970s, police and political pressures impacted the French/Turkish heroin trade, so the drug syndicates needed to find new sources of heroin and make new distribution networks.

THE first phase of selective drug prohibition that began in the late 19th century was then bolstered and reinvigorated anew with the **WAR ON DRUGS**, begun post-WW2 and formalized and expanded by the Nixon administration in tandem with the United Nations. As it did during the first few rounds of drug interdiction efforts before, the updated policing activities and illegalization made the problem worse, increasing production, consumption, and addiction.

Starting after WW2, the UN established a series of conventions expanding drug enforcement globally, increasing the number of prohibited drugs from 17 in 1931 to 245 by 1995. This partnership between the UN and the USA is what established international drug policy for the rest of the world.

While the USA began its own formal anti-drug initiatives in the 1940s, it had already seen a lot of corruption and problems over the previous few decades when attempting to mitigate the drug trade. The first US anti-narcotics agency, the Treasury's Narcotic Division, collapsed in 1929 due to corruption. The US government then created the Federal Bureau of Narcotics (FBN), which itself would collapse in the 1960s due to corruption and criminal behavior, being rebranded as the now infamous Drug Enforcement Agency (DEA) in the 1970s. The FBN was run by a key figure in modern drug law enforcement, Harry J. Anslinger. Anslinger was instrumental in the USA's war on marijuana, helping to push forward the Marihuana Tax Act of 1937, which was the beginning of the criminalization of marijuana. This act was, in fact, an attempt to repress black citizens during the Great Depression, who just happened to use marijuana.

It's important to note that Anslinger was instrumental in establishing the Office of Strategic Services (OSS) during

WW2, which was the forerunner of the CIA. This close connection between anti-drug crusaders and CIA-aligned compatriots is precisely what led to the modern state of the drug war. Anslinger was quick to blame drug smuggling on Communists, which was not usually the case, but this served his political objectives. If drugs were connected to Communists, then funding would be easy to come by, as well as a lack of regulation and oversight.

For instance, it was the French in their war in Indochina and Vietnam in the 1950s that built up and expanded centralized opium production in Southeast Asia. But Anslinger did not blame the French. Without any evidence, he pointed the finger at Vietnam's Communists. Eventually, President Kennedy forced Anslinger into retirement, and by 1973, his FBN was no more, now rebranded into the more public-friendly DEA. But it is important to remember that the DEA always defers to the CIA whenever their covert operations are mixed with the drug war. In other words, US covert operations took precedence and priority over US drug interdiction efforts. While DEA agents were busting lower-level drug smugglers, the CIA was giving money, supplies, arms, and logistics to the drug lord bosses who ran their operations—quite the incestuous situation.

It was in the early 1970s that the War on Drugs took on new life and new branding under President Richard Nixon as he launched a major expansion in US international drug enforcement. Nixon, at the time, was looking to suppress uprisings from black Americans as well as hold down popular opinion by leftists and student activists on the Vietnam War, and making drugs like heroin, marijuana, and LSD highly illegal was a great way to criminalize your political opponents.

One decade after Nixon's War on Drugs, President Ronald Reagan redirected the drug war away from heroin from

Southeast Asia and towards cocaine manufacturing and smuggling in Central and South America. Seeing as our political objectives were now focused on securing our Central American colonies from popular uprisings and elected leftists in the 1980s, this makes sense. Between 1981 and 1994, funds for supply-side suppression of coca plants (raw material for cocaine) represented 80% of America's anti-drug effort. Little money or focus was ever put on treatment or education.

In 1996, President Clinton expanded the War on Drugs yet again, implementing President George Bush's mandate on drug criminalization.

"We must reduce drug use for one great moral reason: illegal drugs are the enemies of ambition and hope. When we fight against drugs, we fight for the souls of our fellow Americans." – President George Bush, 2002

It is important to note that during this time, illegal drugs just became drugs, and by doing this, you will notice Bush is equating marijuana with heroin and cocaine. All illicit drugs are immoral according to moral men like him. Apparently, except when the CIA needs them to fund covert operations, they can be tolerated. And remember when we had to partner with drug dealers to fight Communism? Since it was so horrible? Well, by the early 90s, Communism was pretty much gone; we claimed to have won, apparently, but the drug operations continued unabated.

What has the US-led worldwide drug war accomplished over this past century? Before the 1990s, the US fought four international drug wars that cost nearly $150 billion (the 2023 cost of the Ukraine War), and the result was that the worldwide opium supply grew 5X from 1,200 tons in 1971 to 6,100 tons in 1999. During the first 15 years that the US tried to eradicate cocaine production in South America, coca production doubled to 600,000 tons in 1999. We spend money and terrorize people to make the drug war and drug use WORSE.

With mandatory maximum sentences for non-violent drug offenders in the US, prison rates soared. For over a century, the US incarceration rate stayed steady at 100 prisoners per 100,000 population. After mandatory drug sentencing, the US incarceration rate grew from 138 out of 100,000 in 1980 to 702 out of 100,000 in 2002. In this, the US has created the world's largest prison population, with no end in sight. Violent criminals and rapists are put on the street, while the vast majority of prisoners are non-violent drug offenders. Non-violent drug offenses now drive and provide fuel and bodies for the for-profit prison industry.

Nowhere in the realm of science or data does the US position on illegal drugs make sense. Based on the data, our efforts do not reduce production; they increase it. Our efforts do not reduce addiction but increase it. Our efforts do not reduce criminalization but increase it.

Our government sees and knows that data, but it keeps going forward with its criminalization of drugs. But why? Well, if you accept the premise that the drug war has nothing to do with public or individual health or well-being and instead is used as a method for generating revenue to increase power and control, then it makes total sense.

THE collapse and selling off of the Soviet Union to private investors and oligarchs shifted the global power structure, leading to a new global power framework in which illegal drug trafficking expanded. New criminal syndicates were created and assisted to grow with the protection and oversight of the CIA and the US government, opening up new smuggling routes through Russia and China.

This power shift and the state of drug prohibition enabled incredible profits from the drug trade, contributing to increasing corruption and increased consumption and addiction globally. In the mid-1990s, a kilo of heroin went from $2,870 wholesale in Pakistan to $290,000 when retailed in America. A kilo of cocaine was about $1,500 wholesale in Bolivia and $110,000 if sold as powder in the US. These are obscene profit margins. Name one business that comes even close. All tax-free! Unless you consider bribes and kickbacks to the DEA and government officials as taxes.

It seems, and this is based on lots of supporting data and evidence, that prohibition not only failed to slow illegal drug traffic but has contributed to increasing the global supply significantly. In fact, eradication efforts have only increased cultivation. The numbers from our own government prove this. After the US spent $1.7 billion to defoliate Colombia's coca crop, production rose 25 percent from 2000 to 2001. Seems pretty cut and dry. All that happens is the growing is displaced to new areas, increasing in size when it does.

From the 1960s through the 1990s, all that the US and UN drug prohibition has done is push the production, processing, and smuggling of illicit drugs back and forth across the three main trafficking areas of the world – the Asian opium zone, the Andes coca belt, and the US/Mexico border.

Prohibition has created one of the world's largest industries in illegal international drug trafficking. By the late 1990s, the UN reported that global drug traffic was a $400 billion industry with 180 million users, or 4.2 percent of the world's adults, and 8 percent of world trade.

The illegal drug trade is a larger market than textiles, steel, or cars.

A worldwide black market this large does not operate without support from the more legitimate elements of society, namely the police, intelligence agencies, and banks. In more extreme states, mafioso and police work hand-in-hand, with the police protecting trafficking from investigation, and suspects giving the police occasional busts to make them look legitimate. Many countries with prominent drug kingpins and operations eventually become narco-mafia states, where the mafia, the government, and the police act as one unit supporting each other.

For example, by 1988, in Pakistan, their heroin industry was growing about $8 billion per year, half of the entire legal economy. Pakistani military intelligence directed the drug traffic, while top drug dealers and kingpins would determine parliamentary elections. By 1994, Mexican cartels were paying annual bribes totaling $460 million (gee, who was being bribed?), and were grossing $30 billion, four times the value of the country's oil exports.

During the 2nd half of the 20th century, drug prohibition created a global illegal economy that funds and provides power and control to criminal syndicates, drug warlords, terrorists, and covert operations for countries like the US and France.

IN 1972, graduate student Alfred McCoy wrote the first account of the US government's active involvement in illegal drug smuggling. *The Politics of Heroin* documents CIA complicity and aid to the Southeast Asian opium/heroin trade. His book, like *The Deconstructing America* series, uses the historical method to probe present-day issues by understanding the past. His book explained how, by the 1970s and 1980s, most of the world's heroin was produced in the Golden Triangle and transported by the United States through its own airline, Air America, which was covertly owned and operated by the CIA.

"It is transported in the planes, vehicles, and other conveyances supplied by the United States. The profit from the trade has been going into the pockets of some of our best friends in Southeast Asia. The charge concludes with the statement that the traffic is being carried on with the indifference, if not the closed-eye compliance, of some American officials, and there is no likelihood of its being shut down in the foreseeable future." – Alfred McCoy.

During the initial interview process, the author met with French intelligence and army commanders, now retired, and learned how they used drugs to fund the French Indochina War of the early 1950s. The officers recounted how they used the opium trade to finance cash-strapped covert operations. They did this by taking over colonial opium monopolies and using them to fund covert operations among the hill tribes of Tonkin and Laos.

In 1955, when the French left Vietnam, the CIA took over their illegal drug smuggling operation, lock, stock, and barrel. Uniformed Vietnamese Navy captains detailed to him the movement of heroin from Laos to Phnom Penh on CIA aircraft and then down the Mekong River to Saigon on Vietnamese Navy ships.

During Mr. McCoy's investigations in Vietnam at the time, he was ambushed by CIA-sponsored Hmong soldiers who tried to kill him and his guides. This is when he found that the CIA's Air America was transporting opium for its Hmong hill tribe allies. This young graduate student was so concerned about what he saw that he called Senator William Fulbright, then the Foreign Relations Committee chair, about his findings. The senator listened to the student and then replied that he had known about the CIA's complicity in drug trafficking for years, but it was hopeless, and nobody could do anything about it. It seems he was right. Now, 50 years later, all this continues unabated with zero accountability.

In response, the CIA attempted to repress the book, intimidated sources, harassed the writer, the FBI tapped his phone, and the IRS audited him. The CIA, of course, was never held accountable by Congress for its actions in drug trafficking or really anything else. They truly operate above the law and society's norms and rules.

McCoy's book focuses on South Asian drug lord Khun Sa, who at his height of power controlled 20,000 troops, ruled over 8,000,000 people, and controlled ½ of the world's heroin supply. This, at the time, was the world's most powerful drug lord, with a larger market share than anyone has had since.

In 1990, U.S. Attorney General Richard Thornburgh reported that prosecutors filed an indictment against the "prince of death", aka Khun Sa, for importing 3,500 pounds of heroin into NYC. The head of the DEA called Khun Sa "the self-proclaimed king of opium" and the "most powerful drug trafficker in the Golden Triangle." This was after President G.W. Bush declared yet another War on Drugs after the U.S.

invaded Panama to arrest "drug lord" General Manuel Noriega, a known CIA informant and partner, to bring him back to the US for trial. More on that later in the book.

When drug lord Khun Sa fell in 1996, the fact that his downfall did not affect or slow the flow of heroin out of the Golden Triangle should tell people all they need to know about the US drug war strategy. Make big news going after high-profile drug lords, ones that were originally supplied and supported by US intelligence, and once they are gone, the drug activities just get shifted to new players. Zero effect on the actual industry, but plenty of PR and propaganda for the government and owner-class oligarchy.

"We only capture a drug lord when he is no longer a drug lord." – Alfred McCoy.

Watch as this pattern gets repeated over and over, large-name drug lords like Pablo Escobar are trotted out and called the villains of the world, and when they are taken down, nothing changes in global drug trafficking. That is because we only take them down when they are no longer of use to the broader needs for power and control, or when they get a little too big for their britches.

It is author McCoy's stated opinion that "the book's overall thesis about CIA complicity in the drug trade has been corroborated by the agency's own sources and, more importantly, by history itself."

The reality of the situation was that it was nation-states and corporations that spent several hundred years running the legal drug business before it ever went underground and became a black market. As part of colonial repression and exploitation, civilized countries like Great Britain got entire civilizations like China hooked on dope so they could profit and gain power and control from it.

Then, once the whole thing started making those civilized nations look bad, they said drugs are bad, and now we will forbid you from doing them, while still helping to run and profit from those operations in the dark markets.

After the opium trade collapsed post-WW2, it was military and intelligence agencies that rebuilt the illegal drug trade to fund their clandestine operations. During the 1950s, the CIA, Thai police, the Nationalist Chinese Army (KMT), and the French Military all adopted policies that allowed Southeast Asia's mass opioid addiction to grow and expand.

According to the U.S. Bureau of Narcotics, by the late 1950s, Southeast Asia accounted for 50% of the world's total opium production.

By the 1980s, as crackdowns on opium grew, since opium smelled so distinctly and an addict could easily get busted, users switched to heroin. That is how the world changed from opium addiction to heroin addiction. Heroin does not smell; opium does. Pretty simple.

The French had initially set up a legal opium market in Vietnam that operated for 80 years and then transferred it to an illicit operation for French intelligence called Operation X. (They love these code names, don't they?) This was during the First Indochina War from 1946-1954, in which the dying French colonial empire was trying to maintain power against native nationalist movements, such as the Viet Minh, during the early stages of the Vietnamese revolution in 1945.

Oh BTW, the Vietnamese, or more specifically the Viet Minh, while supported by the Hmong gorillas, kicked the French military's ass in 1954 at their so-called impenetrable fortress. This forced the French to sit down in Geneva and negotiate with those subhuman Asian people they thought so little of.

The French had already set up a nice opium drug smuggling network in Vietnam; now the CIA came in and just picked it up. In fact, the French called the Americans and offered their entire paramilitary apparatus to them, and we accepted. Thanks, guys! Oppressors really look out for each other.

The US ignored the peace agreement that France and Vietnam signed at Geneva and sent in troops and support to create the state of South Vietnam in the mid-1950s. The US thought we could force American beliefs and values on the Vietnamese people, and they would rise to join our side, not the Communists.

"I took my American beliefs with me into these Asian struggles, as Tom Paine would have done." – General Edward Lansdale, CIA tactician.

In other words, the Americans approached Vietnam as Christian Crusaders. Do as I say, not as I do.

Within only 7 years, the guy the US propped up to create South Vietnam and fight the Communists, President Diem, was brought down by a CIA-engineered coup and assassination. It seems the only people who do worse than enemies of the US are its friends.

Opium warlords in Southeast Asia used CIA resources, including arms, ammunition, and mainly air transport to move drugs at an industrial scale, allowing them to increase power and control over their respective communities. The CIA fully embraced and supported regional drug lords and actively enabled them to increase their power with its support. In the end, as the drug warlords' power from opium profits increased, so did the CIA's combat and influence capacities.

The French/CIA both helped to elevate gangsters and criminals to the highest levels of Southeast Asian society so they could be used against the Communists in the power struggle. These gangsters, just like the ones in the USA, were involved in extortion, racketeering, prostitution, drugs, really whatever.

As far as the CIA and the US government were concerned, any method was OK as long as it produced results beneficial to the US elite interests. This is essentially a *Don't Ask, Don't Tell* policy in terms of moral or ethical complicity in criminal activity.

By 1973, twenty years after the CIA first began supporting KMT troops following the Chinese Communist Revolution, in the *Golden Triangle,* the KMT produced 1/3 of the entire world's opium supply, thanks to the support, airpower, and funding of the CIA and US government.

It really was the fall of the nationalist Chinese government to a Communist revolution that set the Golden Triangle in motion as the world's major opium/heroin supplier. The US/Truman administration sent in support and arms to the exiled government hiding out in Burma. The US government established the *Golden Triangle* trade zone to fund its military operations.

All thanks to US intervention, Southeast Asia became the source of 70% of the world's illicit opium supply and a major supplier of raw material for America's growing heroin market.

BY 1968-1969, the Golden Triangle was harvesting close to 1000 tons of raw opium annually, exporting morphine base to European heroin labs, and shipping the drugs to Hong Kong so they could be exported to the US.

In September 1970, army medical officers found that 12% of GIs had tried heroin since they arrived in Vietnam, and almost 7% were still using regularly. By mid-1971, it was estimated that about 10-15% of lower-ranking troops were heroin users. In some commands, the rate was higher at 15-20%. (Those must have been the really shitty assignments)

Why did so many GIs switch to heroin from less harmful drugs like marijuana? Simple. Just like opium, marijuana could be smelled easily. Heroin has no smell, and it is easier to hide. And the fact that heroin was so readily available in large quantities, thanks to the CIA!

And even more fun is the fact that the people who were addicting our GIs were our allies running South Vietnam. Why would they do that? To the tune of $88 million a year in illicit revenue, that is why. In the July 1971 edition of NBC Nightly News, it was announced that the South Vietnamese government was financing its election campaigns with money from narcotics trafficking.

Who did our GIs actually buy their drugs from? From South Vietnamese military officers, that is who. According to one GI, "You can always get some from an ARVN; not a Pfc., but the officers. I've gotten it from as high as Captain." Throughout 1971, unlimited quantities of heroin were available near every US installation in South Vietnam.

In Vietnam, by 1973, 34% of American soldiers had commonly used heroin.

And if you were a GI who got hooked on heroin by your South Vietnamese buddies? Tough shit. Despite President Nixon's promise that "all our servicemen must be accorded the right to rehabilitation," between 1,000 and 2,000 GI addicts per month were being discharged, with zero support for follow-up treatment. What happens to all those addicts when they go home? They kept being heroin addicts, and now the US mafia has a lot of new customers to keep selling Golden Triangle heroin to them, with the support and funding of the CIA.

"Veterans Administration hospitals have handled only three referrals out of 12,000 servicemen on heroin…in Vietnam," – Chairman of the House Subcommittee on Public Health, 1971

It's essential to keep in mind that drug smuggling wasn't all that was going on in Vietnam. Overall, the entire operation was one big money laundering scheme, just like Ukraine is now, in which US taxpayer wealth is washed through a foreign country so it can be redistributed to the wealthy through the military-industrial complex.

And now, if you look at Ukraine, they are taking it to the next level, selling their country off to Blackstone, which will be responsible for rebuilding the country that was leveled by American bombs. Charming little process. They profit from the destruction and the rebuilding of entire societies. Sounds similar to the loop of hooking people on dope and then criminalizing them for it.

When the US withdrew from Vietnam in 1973-1974, the Vietnamese economy went into crisis since it was totally dependent on US funding and goods. They lost 300,000 jobs and saw a whole economic crisis when the US cut military aid to Vietnam by one-half.

By 1975, the corrupt and unsupported South Vietnamese regime was easily overrun by the North Vietnamese, who took the 4-million-person capital of Saigon, with its 300,000 unemployed, 150,000 heroin addicts, and 130,000 prostitutes. Nice work, America! The Crusaders have left the building.

Within months, the Communists set up a New Youth College, a residential drug center with 1,200 beds, and a treatment program using acupuncture, martial arts, and Communist indoctrination. By 1981, the drug program had established an 80% cure rate.

THE first part of the book looked at the origins of the international drug trade, which began with opium and quickly escalated to include heroin and other synthetic, corporate-manufactured substances. This trade system was and is intimately linked to colonialism, the Cold War, clandestine operations, and organized crime. Much of the post-WW2 world was shaped by the interactions among these forces.

And while highly addictive drugs like opium and heroin were perfect to enslave large populations of people to subjugate for the exploitation of wealth and labor, our intelligence leaders saw other types of drugs as potential agents to be used to control an individual's mind directly.

Psychedelic drugs, just like medicinal drugs like opium, had been around for thousands of years and were used in a more religious or spiritual capacity than narcotics before their illegalization. In many world religions, psychedelic drugs like Peyote are still used as sacraments today.

But it was not until the 20th century that psychedelic drugs were supposedly 'rediscovered' by the West, as discoveries like LSD and their use by spy agencies like the CIA in covert operations and unwitting test subjects helped to spread psychedelic drug use and culture across the USA and the world, shaking the very foundations of society.

DR. Albert Hofmann first synthesized LSD (lysergic acid diethylamide) in 1938. He was investigating the chemical and pharmacological properties of ergot, a rye fungus that contains medicinal alkaloids, while working for Sandoz Laboratories in Basel, Switzerland.

In 1977, when famous American poet Allen Ginsberg was on his way to see Dr. Hofmann speak, he opined the following,

"Am I, Allen Ginsberg, the product of one of the CIA's lamentable, ill-advised, or triumphantly successful experiments in mind control? Had the CIA, "by conscious plan or inadvertent Pandora's Box, let loose the whole LSD fad on the U.S. and the world?"

Was Allen Ginsberg correct? Did the CIA, in trying to control the minds of individuals in illegal and unethical experiments, unleash LSD onto the world, helping to destabilize the very system they were trying to preserve? I believe this is accurate, and the evidence only supports this assertion.

Around the same time in 1977, the Senate Subcommittee on Health and Scientific Research, chaired by Ted Kennedy, claimed they were attempting to get to the bottom of Operation **MK-ULTRA**, a secret CIA program in mind control. Testimony was all rehearsed beforehand, so no surprises would be had.

David Rhodes, a former CIA psychologist, told of a failed LSD experiment at a CIA safehouse in San Francisco, in which unsuspecting people in bars were lured to a party where CIA operatives planned to dose everyone at the party, unknowingly to them, using an aerosol spray. Philip Goldman, a CIA chemical warfare specialist, recounted a test in which they coated a swizzle stick with LSD to dose bar patrons. Dr. Sidney Gottlieb, the man who ran the MK-ULTRA program, explained it was "to investigate whether and how it was possible to modify an individual's behavior by covert means."

Another report, confirmed by Dr. Gottlieb, said that prostitutes were used in the safehouse experiments to spike the drinks of unknowing customers while CIA operatives observed, photographed, and recorded the results. Gottlieb claimed the MK-ULTRA program was a reaction to mind control experiments being run in the Soviet Union and China on LSD, of which no evidence has been found to this day.

In the end, the hearings weren't a very serious affair, intended to provide the impression of investigation and accountability without anyone being held accountable. We call this performative. It later emerged that some of the witnesses conferred among themselves and agreed to limit their testimony to the minimum necessary to answer the committee's questions.

Around this time, due to a Freedom of Information Act (FOIA) request by researcher John Marks, documents relating to Operation MK-ULTRA and other CIA mind control projects were available for study, albeit heavily redacted and hard to discover. As researchers dug into the material, they uncovered CIA documents describing experiments in sensory deprivation, sleep teaching, ESP, subliminal projection, electronic brain stimulation, and other methods for behavioral modification.

One program, reminiscent of *The Manchurian Candidate*, was designed to turn people into programmed assassins who would kill on triggered command. The CIA also studied the effects of magnetic fields, ultrasonic vibrations, and other forms of radiant energy on the brain. A quote from a CIA doctor said,

"We lived in a never-never land of 'eyes only' memos and unceasing experimentation." Sounds like fun, huh? Well, maybe for them.

Every drug that appeared on the black market during the 1960s, including marijuana, coke, heroin, shrooms, uppers, and downers, had all been tested and, in some cases, refined by the CIA and Army scientists. But it was LSD that the CIA loved, and in the 1950s, they thought LSD was the key to mind control and a new age of spying.

It all started in 1942, when the head of the Office of Strategic Services (OSS), the organization that would become the CIA after WW2, brought together about six very important people and told them he wanted to develop a speech-inducing drug for use in intelligence interrogations.

The important people he was giving direction to were Dr. Windfred Overhulser, Superintendent of Saint Elizabeth Hospital in Washington, DC, Dr. Edward Strecker, President of the American Psychiatric Association, and Harry J. Anslinger, head of the Federal Bureau of Narcotics (forerunner of the DEA) and the man solely responsible for America's War on Marijuana.

This committee of doctors, psychiatrists, and law enforcement officers worked together to find out what drugs could be used to make people easier to control. They decided to use a synthetic liquid form of marijuana as their speech-inducing agent. The liquid was odorless and tasteless, so it could be injected into other substances without the subject knowing. The marijuana liquid was named TD, short for truth drug. Its effects were listed in an OSS report:

"TD appears to relax all inhibitions and to deaden the areas of the brain which govern an individual's discretion and caution. It accentuates the senses and makes manifest any strong characteristics of the individual. Sexual inhibitions are lowered, and the sense of humor is accentuated to the point where any statement or situation can become extremely funny to the subject."

Unfortunately, marijuana proved to be unreliable in making someone talk. Some people chatted to no end, while others got paranoid and said nothing. Eventually, they gave up on pot as a truth drug. An OSS document stated, "The drug defies all but the most expert and searching analysis, and for all practical purposes can be considered beyond analysis." I guess the intelligence, medical, and psychiatric leadership of America would need to look beyond marijuana for a drug to control people.

Next up in the mind control game was the Navy, with Project CHATTER in 1947, the same year the CIA was founded out of the ashes of the OSS. CHATTER was described as an 'offensive' program; its goal was to obtain information from people, independent of their volition, but without physical duress. Dr. Charles Savage, working for the Navy program, conducted experiments with the psychedelic compound mescaline, a drug similar to LSD, at the Naval Medical Research Institute in Bethesda, Maryland. They used both animal and human subjects and found it was not an effective truth serum; the program ended in 1953.

The Navy decided to use mescaline as an interrogation agent when American investigators learned of mind control experiments done by Nazi doctors at Dachau, where they gave POWs mescaline without their consent or knowledge. All the way back to WW2 and soon after, the U.S. government, at its highest levels, was experimenting with psychedelic drugs to affect the mind, in illegal experiments on unwitting test subjects.

And please don't think for a second the US government and its leaders were too offended by Nazism and its abhorrent fascist ideology, since after WW2 they imported 600 top Nazi scientists under a program named Project PAPERCLIP, supervised by the CIA. Among the charming Nazi individuals who were brought in and given the highest positions in the US research infrastructure were Dr. Hubertus Strunghold, who was directly involved in the mescaline experiment in Dachau and accused of all sorts of horrific atrocities and war crimes. He eventually settled in Texas and became a leader in the U.S. Space Program. NASA hailed him as the 'father of space medicine." Nice people that lead us, huh?

THE CIA continued the OSS program in mind control into the early 50s. But the program was no longer just targeted at foreign spies or war prisoners; it was also targeted at the US domestic population, as was exposed in redacted CIA documents. The CIA wanted to expand the research program in mind control, so it established contact with the research sections of police departments and criminologist laboratories; medical practitioners; professional hypnotists; and psychiatrists who were brought in as paid consultants, while different branches of the military provided varying levels of assistance.

Once this whole apparatus was in place, the program was made official and given a code name, **BLUEBIRD**. Due to the sensitivity of the project and the fact that the CIA was engaged in illegal domestic clandestine activities, the usual channels of authorization were bypassed, and it was funded directly by the CIA director with hidden funds. One CIA document identified this program as highly confidential and said BLUEBIRD material was "not fit for public consumption." Gee, why not?

Do you think American citizens at the time would be concerned that our intelligence, medical, psychiatric, and law enforcement communities were colluding together to research mind control techniques on the general public? How does this program align with what the CIA was just created to do, which is to gather intelligence outside the USA's border to combat Communism? From the onset, the CIA was involved in illegal and illicit activities, and there was no one to hold them accountable for their actions.

How do we know the CIA created BLUEBIRD to try and control American citizens? From the CIA itself. In a memo dated July 13, 1951, it describes the CIA mind-control efforts as —

"Broad and comprehensive, involving both **domestic** and overseas activities, and taking into consideration the programs and objectives of other departments, principally the military services."

BLUEBIRD activities were designed to create an "exploitable alteration of personality" in selected individuals; specific targets included "potential agents, defectors, refugees, POWs, and **others**. I guess **others** means the U.S. population. In August of 1951, BLUEBIRD changed its name to Operation ARTICHOKE.

All this behavior is very fascinating, considering it comes from an organization whose main lobby in Langley, VA, is inscribed with the following words.

"And ye shall know the Truth and the Truth shall set you free."

No more ironic and contradictory words have ever been uttered.

The CIA tried a bunch of other illicit substances looking for a truth drug during BLUEBIRD/ARTICHOKE. They include morphine, ether, cocaine, Benzedrine, ethyl alcohol, heroin, and goofballs (uppers mixed with downers). The CIA sent agents around the world to look for indigenous substances used in tribal ceremonies, too.

Then, in the early 1950s, the CIA came upon the drug that they thought was the solution to their search for the ultimate truth drug, **LSD-25**. One CIA officer said, "We had thought at first that this was the secret that was going to unlock the universe." In fact, the CIA liked acid so much that they referred to agents who were familiar with LSD as **enlightened operatives**. Security officials proposed that LSD be administered to CIA trainee volunteers to see how they would handle the drug and how prone they were to negative effects. The ARTICHOKE steering committee approved this recommendation on November 19, 1953.

Once CIA agents started tripping out on acid themselves to see its effects, things got even weirder. While the initial search was for a truth drug to be used in interrogations, its scope widened quickly as enlightened operatives began to believe that mind control techniques could be applied to a wide range of operations beyond the category of "special interrogation." CIA documents indicate that LSD was employed as an aid to interrogation on an operational basis from the mid-1950s through the early 1960s.

THE CIA needed scientists to study LSD for their mind control experiments. With their hefty budget, the CIA started a series of grants for LSD research through CIA-linked conduits or **cutouts,** including The Geschickter Fund for Medical Research, The Society for the Study of Human Ecology, and The Josiah Macy, Jr. Foundation.

Some key doctors who pioneered LSD research in the USA were the CIA's biggest grant recipients. Dr. Max Rinkel and Dr. Robert Hyde organized an LSD study at the Boston Psychopathic Institute, an early mental health clinic affiliated with Harvard University. Dr. Paul Hoch was another prominent psychiatrist who would offer his services to the CIA.

The CIA funded unorthodox and ethically questionable LSD research by Dr. Ewen Cameron, President of the Canadian, American, and World Psychiatric Associations. Nine of Cameron's former patients have sued the American government for $1,000,000 each, claiming that they still suffer traumatic effects. None of them agreed to be in the LSD experiments. They were all unwilling and unknowing subjects.

It seems that experimenting on unknowing American citizens is a comfortable pastime of the medical elite establishment in the USA.

Through all this, the CIA violated the Nuremberg Code for medical ethics by sponsoring experiments on unwitting subjects. Ironically, Dr. Cameron was a member of the Nuremberg Tribunal that heard Nazi war crime cases, including medical crimes. The hypocrisy is staggering.

And just like the Dachau Nazi doctors whom they followed in their mescaline experiments, the CIA victimized and used vulnerable groups who could not fight back as unwilling test subjects in their experiments, including prisoners, the mentally ill, the terminally ill, LGBTQ, and ethnic minorities.

Dr. Paul Hoch, who later became the New York State Commissioner for Mental Hygiene, performed a series of experiments that involved giving LSD to psychiatric patients and then lobotomizing them to compare the effects of LSD on the brain before and after surgery. In another experiment, LSD was provided with a local anesthetic, and the subject was told to describe his visual experiences as surgeons removed pieces of his cerebral cortex.

Hoch, a doctor who is supposed to care for his patients, commented,

"It is possible that a certain amount of brain damage is of therapeutic value."

Wow. I want you to process that for a second. A doctor claims that giving people brain damage from experimental surgery could be of benefit to the patient.

The Addiction Research Center of the US Public Health Service Hospital in Lexington, Kentucky, a place supposedly for heroin addicts to get clean, was actually a penitentiary. This center was one of 15 penal and mental institutions used by the CIA in its mind control drug development program. The CIA concealed its role by getting help from the Navy and the National Institutes of Mental Health (NIMH), which served as conduits for channeling money to Dr. Harris Isbell, a research scientist who was on the CIA payroll. According to the CIA's own documents, the directors of NIMH and the National Institute of Health (NIH) were both aware of the CIA's connection to Isbell and fully supported the work and relationship.

Whenever the CIA came across a new drug it wanted to test on American citizens, they would send it to Isbell. Over 800 drugs were sent to Isbell for testing on the inmates…ahem…patients. At Lexington under Isbell, patients were rewarded with heroin or morphine if they participated in the CIA drug experiments. Lexington, not coincidentally, had a 90% return rate. Seems the drug addicts really liked the *treatment* they were getting.

CIA documents detail how Dr. Isbell gave black inmates LSD for 75 consecutive days, increasing dosage daily to overcome tolerance. One noted partner of Dr. Isbell's was Dr. Carl Pfeiffer, a pharmacologist who tested LSD on inmates at the federal prison in Atlanta and the Bordentown Reformatory in New Jersey.

How are you feeling about America's leading doctors and scientists after hearing this? Is it starting to make more sense how they reacted during the COVID-19 pandemic? Not in the public interest, but by sending the public up the river while supporting their handlers in the corporate oligarchy and pharmaceutical industry.

Dr. Isbell was very busy. He also served as a go-between for the CIA to get drug samples from European pharmaceutical makers, who thought they were supplying medicine to a public health official. The CIA, in turn, acted as a research coordinator between LSD research scientists, passing along information and tips, so they could be kept abreast of any developments. So helpful of them. They must really care about science.

All of the doctors mentioned in this section, including Isbell, Pfeiffer, Cameron, West, and Hoch, were part of a network of doctors and scientists who willingly gathered information for the CIA. They reported back to the CIA on other doctors engaging in LSD research. During this period, the CIA monitored ALL LSD research in the USA and attempted to keep an eye on global research. The FDA worked closely with the CIA, where the FDA acted in a supervisory role in distributing LSD to American investigators for MK-ULTRA experiments.

Arthur Stoll, President of Sandoz, the Swiss company that manufactured LSD, agreed to keep the CIA posted whenever new LSD was produced or shipped to a customer, and any information on LSD research behind the Iron Curtain would be passed along as well.

It seems a very cozy relationship exists at the highest levels between the military, intelligence, scientists, doctors, and pharmaceutical companies, who are all happy to work together on illegal and illicit programs intended to manipulate and harm American citizens.

IN 1953, with the appointment of new CIA Director Allen Dulles (read the excellent book *The Devil's Chessboard* on Dulles), the CIA formalized and expanded its mind control programs. On April 10, 1953, at Princeton University during the National Alumni Conference, Dulles commented on "how sinister the battle for men's minds had become in Soviet hands." Dulles said the human mind was a malleable tool, and the USSR had secretly developed "brain perversion techniques."

It is to be noted that not then, nor any time in the future, not even after the fall of the U.S.S.R., has any evidence ever been found that the USSR was in fact engaged in mind control experimentation like the U.S. government was involved in.

Three days after making these completely false and fantastical statements, Dulles authorized Operation MK-ULTRA, the CIA's Cold War drug and mind control program, which evolved out of Project ARTICHOKE. MK-ULTRA was the brainchild of Richard Helmes, a high-ranking member of the CIA's dirty tricks department, and was run by an internal CIA group named the Technical Services Staff (TSS).

Dr. Sidney Gottlieb, the chemist who ran MK-ULTRA, had approved a plan to give LSD to unwitting American citizens to see how they would react in a real-world setting. To prepare for this experiment, CIA operatives began secretly dosing each other to see how they would respond. A plan to put LSD in the punch at the annual CIA Christmas office party was canceled as too dangerous. Many experiments unsurprisingly went awry.

In November 1953, Dr. Gottlieb and a group of CIA and Army technicians spent a weekend at a hunting lodge. Dr. Gottlieb spiked everyone's drinks with LSD and told them so afterward. One scientist, Dr. Frank Olson, had a bad reaction to the LSD and went psychotic. Several weeks later, he jumped out of a window; many suspect the agency had him suicided. The circumstances surrounding his death were covered up for some time.

For the next phase of his experiments, Gottlieb enlisted the help of Harry Anslinger, Chief of the Federal Narcotics Bureau (FBN), the forerunner of the DEA, to get a narcotics man, George Hunter White, to run the *LSD in a real-world* operation.

As part of this program, George Hunter White rented an apartment in New York's Greenwich Village and, with CIA funding, made it into a safehouse with two-way mirrors and surveillance equipment. White posed as an artist, lured people back to his apartment, and dosed them with LSD without them knowing.

Then, in 1955, White went to San Francisco, where he set up two more safehouses. He then initiated *Operation Midnight Climax* (boy, they sure love their code names, don't they?), in which he hired drug-addicted prostitutes to pick men up from local bars and bring them back to a CIA-funded whorehouse with two-way mirrors, dosing them unknowingly with LSD and recording them. The hookers received $100 a night and a guarantee that White would help them if they got arrested for anything.

These experiments on the general public by the CIA using LSD continued unabated for eight more years until 1963, when CIA inspector general John Earman accidentally found out about the program during an inspection of operations. He immediately saw that the program was potentially "distasteful and unethical" and wrote a lengthy report on it for the new CIA director. Earman said the LSD safehouse experiments put "the rights and interests of U.S. citizens in jeopardy." He further noted that LSD had been tested on "individuals at all social levels, high and low, native American and foreign." Perhaps the worst crime of all. Many subjects had become ill, and some required hospitalization for days or weeks afterward. But not to worry, more level heads prevailed, as the leadership of the CIA squashed the report and the LSD safehouse program continued another three years until at least 1966, when White left the DEA/CIA.

George Hunter White commented on his time working for the CIA in a letter to Gottlieb,

"I was a very minor missionary, actually a heretic, but I toiled wholeheartedly in the vineyards because it was fun, fun, fun. Where else could a red-blooded American boy lie, kill, cheat, steal, rape, and pillage with the sanction and blessing of the All-Highest?"

Sounds like a nice guy, huh?

During the late 50s and into the mid-60s, LSD was deployed in covert operations by the CIA. LSD was now code-named *P-i* when used operationally, and one of the proposed uses was to dose Communist, Socialist, or left-leaning politicians in foreign countries so they would babble incoherently in public and discredit themselves. Yes, this is what our government was researching LSD-25 for.

WHILE the CIA was primarily concerned with using LSD in cloak-and-dagger applications, the U.S. Army wanted to use the chemical as a biological warfare agent. They saw LSD as a madness gas where they could dose an entire city before an invasion, making the enemy compliant and harmless. They could accomplish this by dosing a city's water supply or releasing the drug in an aerosol form. Congress and the Joint Chiefs approved this concept to begin studies to operationalize the plan. Major General William Creasy, Chief Officer of the U.S. Army Chemical Corps, during his congressional testimony, called for the testing of hallucinogenic gases on subways in American cities. Thankfully, that part of the plan was not approved. Whew.

During the 1950s, the Army conducted extensive in-house studies, as well as funding research at universities and civilian hospitals, with LSD. EA-1729 was the Army's secret code for LSD. LSD was given to soldiers to see how well they would manage in typical military situations. Other tests were conducted, which included giving soldiers LSD while in sensory deprivation tanks and being subject to hostile questioning.

After the tests, the military began using LSD as an interrogation agent in an operational capacity, just as the CIA was already doing. This is confirmed by an Army memo from September 6, 1961, "Stressing techniques employed included silent treatment before or after EA-1729 administration, sustained conventional interrogation before EA-1729 interrogation, deprivation of food, drink, sleep, or bodily evacuation, sustained isolation before EA-1729 administration, hot-cold switched in approach, duress pitches, verbal degradation and bodily discomfort, or dramatized threats to subject's life or mental health."

By the mid-1960s, over 1500 military personnel had served as guinea pigs in LSD experiments run by the US Army Chemical Corps. Some of these subjects later said they were coerced into volunteering by their superior officers. Some said they suffered severe depression and emotional issues following exposure to LSD. Even so, many Army soldiers enjoyed LSD and began stealing it and using it for recreational purposes.

Army scientists coined the term TRIP to describe an LSD experience during these formative years.

In the late 50s, the Army found another super hallucinogen drug that made LSD look like child's play. A drug called quinuclidinyl benzilate, or BZ, has the codename EA-2277. A BZ trip lasted for three whole days, with symptoms including headaches, giddiness, disorientation, auditory and visual hallucinations, and maniacal behavior. For some people, the trip would last for as long as 6 weeks.

Testing on BZ began in 1959 and continued until 1975. During that time, 2,800 soldiers were exposed. Military personnel have come forward and said they were never the same after taking BZ. During the early 1960s, the CIA and military began phasing out their acid tests in favor of BZ, which became the army's standard incapacitating agent. BZ was weaponized and could be delivered in the air or through standard munitions and bombs. BZ was alleged to have been used in Vietnam during the insurgency by American troops. Oh, and according to a CIA document, there was also a contingency plan to use BZ on the US population for civilian insurrection.

"We will use these things as we very well see fit, when we think it is in the best interest of the US and their allies." – General from the Army Chemical Corps.

THE ACID LEAK

WHEN LSD first started leaking out to the public it was through students like Ken Kesey who were involved in CIA-sponsored research programs. It was also given to writers like Aldous Huxley directly by the CIA and to actors like Cary Grant through early psychedelic therapy.

In May 1953, one month into the formal MK-ULTRA program, Aldous Huxley, author of *Brave New World*, was given mescaline by a doctor connected to the CIA's LSD experiments. He wrote a book called *The Doors of Perception* about it. This is also where the name for the rock band *The Doors* came from. Huxley's most famous work *Brave New World* envisions a future totalitarian society in which the world controllers chemically dope up the population into loving their own servitude. Huh, does this sound like a country you may be familiar with based on my books?

Allen Ginsberg was an MK-ULTRA test participant in 1959. Other famous people who were turned on through the government's LSD drug programs include Andre Previn, Jack Nicholson, James Coburn, and Lord Buckley.

Ken Kesey, the writer who wrote the great American masterpiece *One Flew Over the Cuckoo's Nest*, wrote much of it under the influence of LSD. While part of the MK-ULTRA program at Stanford University he snuck some acid out and shared it with his friends. He then created an LSD-oriented art group called *The Merry Pranksters* and ran *Acid Test* parties on the West Coast, with their famous bus ride across the USA in 1964 tripping and spreading the word of LSD across straight America. The Grateful Dead were the house band at these early acid parties.

"Before I took drugs, I didn't know why the guys in the psycho ward at the VA Hospital were there. I didn't understand them. After I took LSD, suddenly I saw it. I saw it all. I listened to them and watched them, and I saw that what they were saying and doing was not so crazy after all." – Ken Kesey

Another notable tripper was the great French Dadaist and Anti-Art provocateur Antonin Artaud. (The cleverer people will note that it is his picture for my profile on https://twitter.com/Power2Control page) He once said of the Peyote experience,

"Once one has experienced a visionary state of mind, one can no longer confuse the lie with truth. One has seen where one comes from and who one is, and one no longer doubts what one is. There is no emotion or external influences that can divert one from this reality."

THE CIA had plenty of assistance from corporate media whom they worked very closely since its inception. This included Henry Luce, President of Time-Life, who acted as chief propagandist for decades of American policy and culture. He openly encouraged his reporters and correspondents to collaborate with the CIA, and his entire publishing empire served as a longtime propaganda asset for the agency.

When the CIA was still high on the potential of LSD, propaganda outlets like *Life Magazine* ran positive stories on magic mushrooms in 1957 that helped to turn the public onto these experiences. Based on these stories, Dr. Hoffman, the inventor of LSD, synthesized psilocybin from the mushrooms. Timothy Leary, a professor studying clinical psychology, read the Life article and it changed his entire research focus to psychedelics.

In 1962 LSD began to fall out of favor with the establishment as the CIA shifted its behavioral research activities towards operations and away from long-range studies. Once they made this shift, the government stopped providing support for LSD researchers and scientists, and LSD was eventually made illegal. The CIA and Army at this point had adopted BZ as their mind control drug. The FDA continued to approve LSD for intelligence and military use while making it illegal for scientists and researchers.

By 1966, the Chairman of the Senate Subcommittee on Juvenile Delinquency (who was in fact an anti-Communist crusader) declared LSD a scourge on America's youth, and worked to demonize and illegalize the drug. It is interesting to note that people like him did not have any problem with LSD when it was being used by the CIA for their purposes.

The following are typical anti-drug scare headlines from the press at the time.

"GIRL 5, EATS LSD AND GOES WILD!"

"THRILL DRUG WARPS MIND, KILLS!"

"A MONSTER IN OUR MIDST – A DRUG CALLED LSD"

One government agent said LSD was "the greatest threat facing the country today…more dangerous than the Vietnam War."

Not just a few years earlier, Henry Luce, President of Life Magazine, had trumpeted the use of psychedelics for all sorts of beneficial applications. Now, according to his publishing empire, taking LSD was a one-way trip to HELL. This is in the space of only about 5 years. Fascinating. How sincere do these people sound to you?

According to Life in 1966, "A person can become permanently deranged through a single terrifying LSD experience. LSD is being dropped into girls' drinks. Terrifying parties are being given a surprise in the punch. The Humane Society is picking up disoriented dogs…"

What happens to journalists and media companies who don't play ball with the CIA and the owner classes? Well, in part three, you will hear about how journalist Gary Webb committed suicide by shooting himself twice in the head after exposing the CIA/Contra drug and arms smuggling ring. Today, we call this getting **Epsteined**.

Or, let's say it's the early 1980s, and you are a big media company like ABC, and you plan to publish a story that will accuse the CIA of attempting to murder US citizens. Well, suppose you are CIA Director William Casey. In that case, you own a media company, Capital Cities, that you founded in 1954, and while you are CIA director, you still control millions of dollars in the company's stock.

In 1984, CIA director Casey asked the FCC to revoke all of ABC's TV and radio licenses in retaliation for an ABC News report that the CIA had attempted to assassinate a US citizen (ABC News, 9/19/84, 9/20/84).

In March 1985, ABC was bought by the media company Cap Cities, owned by CIA Director William Casey, for $43.4 billion. (Read *The Seizing of the American Broadcast Company* by Andy Boehm, LA Weekly, 2/20-26/87).

See, it's pretty simple. If the US media gets out of line and talks about things it's not supposed to, there are several methods for correcting their misalignment. First is an executive action, aka assassination, of the questionable parties, like Gary Webb. Second is financial pressure, like just buying out entire media companies when they threaten the power structure.

THINGS got even weirder during the mid to late 60s as the CIA now tried to undermine (or did they?) the very trend and social explosion they had helped to promote and create through their unethical and illegal experiments on the unwitting American public.

According to doctors who worked at the Haight-Ashbury Free Clinic during the late 60s, there was a series of adverse reactions when a mysterious compound called synthetic THC was introduced to the community. The drug in question was actually phencyclidine (PCP), also called Angel Dust, which was initially marketed as an animal tranquilizer by Parke-Davis in the late 1950s.

Hmm. It seems every single illegal nightmare drug we have been warned about was originally marketed and sold as a medication by pharmaceutical companies. It also appears the Army was testing PCP on American GIs at the Edgewood Arsenal in the late 1950s. At the same time, PCP was given to psychiatric patients at the Allain Memorial Institute in Montreal under Operation MK-ULTRA. The CIA later stockpiled PCP for use as a 'nonlethal incapacitant,' although they did acknowledge high doses could lead to convulsions and death.

So, did the CIA knowingly insert PCP into the LSD ghettos of the '60s as a way to control and harm those troublesome hippies that they disliked so much? Most of the files of MK-ULTRA have been destroyed, so we have no way of knowing the real scope of the project.

At the same time, the original hippie LSD manufacturers like Stanley Owsley (Bear) were no longer the primary source of acid on the streets. Now the mafia came in (remember the mafia? The good friends and partners of the CIA) to sell black-market, low-quality LSD on the streets, typically laced with speed or strychnine. And what was the CIA up to at this time?

According to a former CIA contract employee, agency personnel helped these very underground mafioso chemists set up LSD laboratories during the Summer of Love to "monitor" events and the hippie community in San Francisco. A CIA agent who claims to have infiltrated the covert LSD network called Haight-Ashbury a 'human guinea pig farm."

Wait one sec, so did the MK-ULTRA operation move into the open public, as they went from safehouses to experimenting on a wider social group to do their mind control experiments? This was the same place where CIA agent George Hunter White set up a safe house and began testing on unwitting citizens a decade-plus earlier. White's safehouse operation was phased out in the mid-60s, perhaps because LSD had gone into the community and the CIA could monitor test subjects in the wild, or, as they say, in field conditions.

In addition to the spies who inserted themselves into relationships with drug chemists and dealers, there were CIA scientists who stationed themselves in the acid communities for monitoring purposes. Dr. Louis Joylon West, an LSD investigator with the CIA, rented an apartment in the heart of Haight-Ashbury with the intention of studying hippies in their native habitat.

ONCE the CIA and Army limited their LSD experimentation and psychedelics overall were made illegal, demand had already been created, and it began to appear on the black market. Huh, remember what happened with opium and heroin? Legitimate organizations created the demand, so illegalization only serves to drive the market underground. The 1960s psychedelic drug revolution had begun, thanks to the U.S. government, the CIA, the Army, corporate media like Time-Life, and lots of colluding scientists and doctors. And as corporate media turned against psychedelics and constantly hyped and focused on negative LSD stories, it invariably increased use and popularity among young people.

Four million Americans are reported to have tried LSD in the late 1960s, with the average user taking a dose every three to four months. 70% of users were of high school or college age. All thanks to our compassionate and empathetic leaders, who care deeply for our youth and their health and well-being.

This, by the way, is the standard playbook for drug illegalization. The government and private enterprises push drugs on people for a variety of objectives (profit, control, etc.), then, when those drugs become embarrassing as they penetrate the upper strata of society, those drugs are vilified and illegalized. At the same time, the lower classes are held accountable for the crimes of their leaders. Charming process.

Oh, and this is around when the perennial, but completely unscientific and unsubstantiated theory, still being used to this day, came about - the **GATEWAY DRUG** theory. This theory says that if you start with lighter drugs like marijuana, you will eventually get hooked on heroin. There is no data to support this propaganda at all. But this chestnut is still being used to this day. And if this logic were in fact true, then wouldn't alcohol be the first actual gateway drug?

All of this control and oversight really only applied to certain drugs used by certain people, which exposes the true purpose and objective of the drug war – Individual and group control.

JUST like with marijuana before it, when the government went after blacks in their ghettos during the 1930s in the depression to keep them in line, during the 1960s, politicians were able to use LSD and hallucinogenic drugs to attack the anti-war movement, calling radicals drug-crazed lunatics who were out of their minds. Labeling dissidents as drug addicts is a great way to mitigate your opposition's effectiveness and criminalize their activities.

"We are now in a position to understand the real reason for the condemnation of hallucinogens and why their use is punished. The authorities do not behave as though they were trying to stamp out a harmful vice, but as though they were attempting to stamp out dissidence. Since this is a form of dissidence that is becoming more widespread, the prohibition takes on the proportion of a campaign against spiritual contagion, against an opinion. What the authorities are displaying is *ideological zeal*; they are punishing a heresy, not a crime."

- Octavio Paz in Alternating Currents

Here, we return to the core thesis of this book. Is the drug war a matter of public health, or is it more about a tool to leverage power and control over disenfranchised groups? All the media and government warnings about drugs like LSD being the worst thing to ever happen to American youth don't hold water with the actual data. It's the legal drugs and substances that are socially and legally tolerated that have the most significant impact on individual and public health.

Today, almost 30 million American citizens are addicted to alcohol. 90% of Americans consume caffeine daily, with tens of millions consuming enough to cause health issues. About 28 million people smoke cigarettes, which, you know, causes lung cancer.

Even with all these horrible drugs out there impacting public health in measurable ways, during his 1968 State of the Union address, President Johnson only mentioned LSD as the need for a war on dangerous drugs. Based on what criteria exactly? The only criterion was that the people using LSD (students, leftists, protesters) were the ones the government wanted to crack down on for political reasons.

Oh, it wasn't just government stooges who were on the anti-LSD craze, but their partners in the media were complicit in creating an atmosphere of paranoia and distrust. It was the media who promoted and pushed LSD usage into the mainstream after the CIA leaked it out into hipper circles just a few years earlier.

In just a few years, LSD was designated Public Enemy Number One by the corporate media, whipping American citizens into a paranoid frenzy over psychedelic drugs. The press put out completely fabricated and false reports of chromosome damage in people from LSD. Tests run by the Army Chemical Corps on the hazards of LSD found no such connection. According to Dr. Van Sim, Chief of Clinical Research at Edgewood Arsenal during the 60s and 70s,

"We were unable to demonstrate any damage by LSD to any system used."

Maybe the squares were right to be afraid of LSD, the CIA's wonder drug, which they unleashed on the American public. In fact, much of the revolutionary fervor of the late 60s was amplified by the widespread use of LSD and other hallucinogens. According to John Sinclair, former head of the White Panther Party –

"When the beatniks started taking acid, it brought us out of the basement, the dark place, the underworld, the fringes of society. LSD gave us the idea that it could be different. We were going to take over the world. Acid was amping up everything, driving everything into greater and greater frenzy."

Like so many other insiders, Mr. Sinclair wondered whether the CIA was behind the whole acid craze. "They're the ones who had it."

This all came to a head at the 1968 Democratic Convention, where 12,000 police and hundreds of undercover agents had gathered, along with 6,000 National Guardsmen, to stop any hippie nonsense or political protests as had been promised by the political Yippie group. The National Guard was in full battle dress, equipped with M-1 rifles, gas masks, and machine guns mounted on military vehicles. The police viciously attacked the nonviolent protesters, clubbing and macing young and old alike, male and female, protesters and bystanders. News reporters and photographers were beaten along with the rest (sounds a lot like BLM), while Army helicopters kept an eye on the horrors unfolding below.

"For me, that week in Chicago was far worse than the worst acid trip I'd even heard rumor about," said Hunter S. Thompson.

Over 1,000 demonstrators had been injured, and National Guard troops killed one student.

"Chicago, I think, was the place where all America was radicalized," said Tom Wicker of the New York Times. "The miracle of television made it visible to all."

Can social unrest during the 60s and the radicalization of US youth be laid anywhere but at the feet of the CIA and corporate media? The revolutionary fever of the 1960s was amplified by the widespread use of LSD and other psychedelics, which were leaked to and promoted for years by these groups. But not to worry, the FBI is an expert at penetrating and undermining left-wing students and workers' organizations, causing so much angst to the ruling elite.

LOCATED at Quantico Marine base in Virginia, *Hoover University* was an elite academy specializing in training FBI agents to infiltrate hippies and left-wing organizations. To create the right image, undercover agents were told not to wash or bathe for several days before infiltrating a group of radicals. Undercover FBI agents smoked marijuana and dropped LSD with unsuspecting hippies and radicals in the field.

According to Army intelligence documents, one out of six demonstrators at the 1968 Democratic Convention in Chicago was an undercover operative.

FBI spies in Chicago included Bob Pierson, a Chicago cop disguised as a biker, who became Jerry Rubin's bodyguard at the convention. Mr. Pierson would always be at the forefront of antagonistic actions, like throwing stones at police, pulling down American flags, leading crowds in militant chants, and urging protesters to start fires and tie up traffic. Interesting. I wonder how many FBI agents used these same tactics to infiltrate Occupy Wall Street or Black Lives Matter and discredit those nonviolent protest movements? It was Agent Pierson's testimony at the trial of the Chicago Seven that put people behind bars until an appeals court overturned their convictions.

The use of informants and agent provocateurs was part of an extensive campaign to subvert political dissent in the 1960s and 1970s. It wasn't just the FBI engaged in these anti-citizen, anti-free speech activities; they joined and worked in full partnership with the IRS, FBN/DEA, FCC, the Department of Health, military intelligence, and local police.

During this period, over 250,000 American citizens were under *active surveillance*, while dossiers were kept on the lawful political activities and personal lives of millions more.

Do you think that perhaps this level of police state surveillance of our own population not only did not stop but continued to be refined through the succeeding decades?

During the Nixon administration, the CIA stepped up its domestic spying and clandestine operations even though the agency's charter outlawed it. In 1969, the CIA created a report called *Restless Youth*, which determined that the New Left and black nationalist movements were a homegrown phenomenon and that foreign ties (aka Communists) to US dissidents were insubstantial. Well, this is not what Nixon and his cronies wanted to hear. For people like that, everything is a Communist conspiracy to be leveraged for political power and control.

Nixon then pressed CIA Director Richard Helms to expand the parameters of this effort, now dubbed **Operation CHAOS**. In addition to monitoring liberal and left-wing organizations, the CIA provided training, technical assistance, exotic equipment, and intelligence data to local police departments. In terms of covert operations, one example of the CIA's tactics included sprinkling itching powder on the public toilets near leftist/populist meetings. Really mature and valid tactics, huh? Is there any scientific or data-based evidence backing these tactics? Or is it really what it looks like? A domestic secret police force that harasses and intimidates the general public.

At the same time, the FBI was escalating its war against all forms of political and cultural dissidents in America. Did you know that was a primary objective of the FBI for nearly a century now? The story of going after bank robbers and sex traffickers is really just a cover story to hide what the FBI really is: a domestic secret police force. One of the FBI's primary goals was to target freedom of expression in the underground press. There was also a campaign to make political arrests by charging radicals with possession of small amounts of marijuana.

"Since the use of marijuana and other narcotics is widespread among members of the New Left, you should be alert to opportunities to have them arrested on drug charges," J. Edgar Hoover stated in a top-secret FBI memo.

"Any information concerning the fact that individuals have marijuana should be immediately furnished to local authorities, and they should be encouraged to take action."

You see, things aren't a conspiracy theory when the authorities themselves are telling you they are doing it.

In concert with these agencies, Nixon made the issue of drug abuse a cornerstone of his political campaign in 1968, vowing to restore law and order to a world gone mad. When Nixon took office, he pushed through a series of no-knock laws that allowed police to break into the homes of suspected drug users fully armed and search for any number of drugs. These anti-drug laws were selectively applied to 60s/70s dissidents and radicals.

For example, in 1969, John Sinclair, leader of the White Panther Party, was sentenced to nine and a half years in prison for giving two marijuana joints to an undercover officer. He did not sell him the joints, mind you. Other examples include Lee Otis Johnson, a black militant and anti-war organizer, who was given a 30-year sentence for sharing a joint with a narc. Police in Buffalo planted weed in a bookstore run by Martin Sostre, a black anarchist who had served six years before

Amnesty International got him out. Drug laws were used to go after Timothy Leary and other counterculture leaders. They were also used for surveillance and to go after musicians involved in political issues, like John Lennon. In addition, the FBI conducted surveillance on Jimi Hendrix, Janis Joplin, Jim Morrison, The Fugs, and many other rock stars at the time.

Much of the negative framing by the press of the New Left was actually due to the activities of undercover FBI agent provocateurs, who posed as radicals and tried to incite others to engage in violence, burn flags, break windows, and whatnot. These tactics are used to discredit non-violent protests to this day.

The level of social disruption during the late 60s cannot be denied. During the spring of 1969, major demonstrations occurred at nearly 300 colleges and universities, involving 1/3 of the nation's students. Where are you today when we need you, young people?

WITH student activities and dissidents protesting against the Vietnam War and police brutality at home, military strategists were working hard on ideas to quell civil unrest, and this included using the new Army psycho-chemical incapacitating super hallucinogen agent BZ against the US population.

The US had already used BZ in Vietnam, according to a 1966 French magazine article, in which grenades containing BZ were deployed against a Vietcong battalion of 500 troops. A Dutch author said BZ was used on at least five other occasions in Vietnam between 1968 and 1970. It was said to be of limited success as an incapacitant. But no worries, the US Army stockpiled 50 tons of BZ at the time, enough to turn the whole world into lunatics. Hmm, wonder if these experiments in suppressing civil unrest in the USA continued and are being used to this day?

According to Army documents, the government was seriously considering using BZ as a domestic riot control technique. One plan they had was to use remote-controlled airplanes called *mechanical bees* (aka drones) to be mounted with syringes that would target select protesters at rallies to inject them with BZ. Another plan called for spraying BZ gas to incapacitate an unruly mob. A CIA memo dated September 4, 1970, said,

"Trends in modern police action and warfare indicate the desire to incapacitate reversibly and demoralize, rather than kill, the enemy…with the advent of highly potent natural products, psychotropic and immobilizing drugs, a new era of law enforcement…is being ushered in."

Today in 2024, how are you all liking these new police tactics? Are you seeing how they have been deployed in recent years to put down large-scale protests like Occupy Wall Street and Black Lives Matter?

IT is this author's opinion, based on everything you have read here, that the 1960s psychedelic drug revolution would not have occurred in the same fashion, in the size and scope it achieved, without the direct intervention of the CIA introducing young people to psychedelics like LSD through the MK-ULTRA program.

It's important to remember it was not the CIA acting alone but in partnership with the corporate media, which initially promoted psychedelic drug use as a positive force, only to turn about-face within five years to disseminate unscientific propaganda campaigns about the horrors of LSD, which in turn only advertised tripping to millions of curious American youths.

More notable names than myself indeed suspect this to be true, even way back then, before so much of this information had come out. Not only that, but they also suspected the CIA continued to push black market LSD onto the streets to weaken the anti-war movement, not strengthen it.

"LSD makes people less competent. You can see their motivation for turning people on. Make it available, and the news media takes it up, and there it is. They don't have to stick out their necks very much." – William S. Burroughs.

"It makes perfect sense to me. We thought at the time that, as a result of our LSD-inspired activities, great things would happen. And, of course, it didn't. They were up there moving shit around. Down on the street, nobody knew what was going on." – John Sinclair.

No truer words about how power and control are wielded in the USA have ever been spoken. They are up there moving things around, stacking the deck, while no one down the chain has a clue about what is really going on.

"You don't hear about it anymore, but people are still visiting the cosmos. We must always remember to thank the CIA and the Army for LSD. That's what people forget. They invented LSD to control people, and what they did was give us freedom. Sometimes it works in mysterious ways, its wonders to perform." – John Lennon, 1980

The use of LSD among young people in the US reached a peak in the late 1960s, shortly after the CIA initiated a series of covert operations designed to disrupt and discredit the New Left. Not to worry, though, according to our bastions of truth and honor, then CIA Director Richard Helms said to the American Society of Newspaper Editors in 1971,

"We do not target American citizens. The nation must, to a degree, take it on faith that we who lead the CIA are honorable men, devoted to the nation's service."

The man who spoke this obscene lie was directly involved with MK-ULTRA and had used unwitting American citizens as guinea pigs in mind control experiments, as well as launched a massive illegal domestic spying campaign against the anti-war movement and dissidents in the US. Upon Helms's departure from the CIA, all drug and mind control project documentation was destroyed on his orders. What little we know about these programs comes from highly redacted material, which was briefly available through FOIA requests.

I am sorry, sir, we do not have faith that you are an honorable man.

AS you will read in part three, things kept escalating with the CIA as it was unleashed by the Reagan administration to become even more of an international dissident police force than before. There would be no comeuppance for the CIA or those who partnered with them in their crimes against humanity.

For example, congressional investigations in the early 1990s found that massive amounts of cash that were intended for Pakistani military officials and Afghan guerrilla leaders were used to grease an arms-for-heroin pipeline in Southeast Asia. Much of this dirty money was laundered through CIA-cutout institutions such as the Bank of Credit and Commerce International (BCCI). Yes, the CIA has its own banks that it uses to wash its criminal buddies' ill-gotten gains.

At the same time in Central America, Lieutenant Colonel Oliver North (you know that name) and high-level CIA officials aided and abetted large-scale cocaine smugglers who were sending weapons to the Nicaraguan Contras, a paramilitary terrorist organization. A Costa Rican court found that North and others were guilty of secretly facilitating narcotic trafficking in Central America, all while the Reagan administration was going on about the War on Drugs and Just Say No and all that nonsense.

And then there was the Invasion of Panama in 1989, when the US went in to stop the evil drug pusher and kingpin General Manuel Noriega, who had in fact been on the CIA payroll for years, according to their own documents. Wait till you hear about how that all goes.

In the succeeding years, multiple victims of CIA drug tests have come forward, seeking compensation for the injuries they sustained. In 1988, nine former psychiatric patients at Allain

Memorial Hospital in Montreal agreed to an out-of-court settlement after suing the CIA and the Canadian government. Guess they were doing this in Canada, too? How many other countries were involved? No apologies came from the CIA or the Canadian government.

A federal judge in Manhattan awarded $700,000 to the family of Harold Blauer, a tennis professional who died during an army chemical warfare experiment. Jim Stanley, another unwitting subject in an army drug test, took his case to the Supreme Court, which in 1987 ruled that enlisted personnel can't sue for injuries related to their service.

So, note to anyone wanting to join the service. They can experiment on you at will without your knowledge, and you have no recourse. Oh, and even more interesting, Jim Stanley was forced to drink a mysterious liquid at Edgewood Arsenal, the Army Chemical Corps' HQ. It was at Edgewood that staff included at least eight Nazi scientists brought over during Operation Paperclip.

Our country brought Nazis back and then allowed them to experiment on our soldiers just like they had done to concentration camp victims at Dachau. Welcome to the real America, folks.

Today, the CIA continues its drug research programs, but now they are smart enough to conduct those tests at universities and research labs in foreign countries. You know, places like Wuhan, China, where the US funds dangerous gain-of-function research on Coronaviruses. Who knows what other advancements in leveraging drugs for power and control they have made over the past few decades? Take a look around at how passive and quiet the public has become since the 60s/70s. Where are the leftist groups? Where are the revolutionaries? Where are the revolutionary publications?

Perhaps a combination of media control, mind control, and social control has all mollified the US population into being subservient and pliable.

A lot of what came out about the CIA occurred during the 1970s in congressional hearings about MK-ULTRA and mind control. These hearings were never meant to be serious or to hold anyone or any group accountable. The hearings were show trials intended to placate the public and convince them that there was, in fact, some oversight of the CIA and US intelligence research and operations.

If there had been any accountability for the CIA and its actions during the 1950s, 60s, and 70s, perhaps some of the events of the 1980s would not have occurred. But there was to be no comeuppance for the CIA or their collaborators. In fact, in the 1980s, they were empowered by the Reagan administration to act in an even more reckless fashion, giving birth to the 1980s crack boom in LA and the rest of the country through their direct and active support of the para-military extremist group **The Contras**, who were, in fact, some of the most ruthless weapon smugglers, drug dealers, and terrorists in the world.

"FOR the better part of a decade, a Bay Area drug ring sold tons of cocaine to the Crips and Bloods street gangs of LA and funneled millions in drug profits to a Latin American guerrilla army run by the U.S Central Intelligence Agency, a Mercury News investigation found. This drug network, federal records show, opened the first pipeline between Colombia's cocaine cartels and the black neighborhoods of LA, a city now known as the crack capital of the world. The cocaine it brought into the US fueled the crack explosion in urban America, and the simultaneous rise to power of the murderous gangs of black LA."

- Gary Webb, author of Dark Alliance: The CIA, The Contras, and the Crack Cocaine Explosion:

In a series of congressional hearings from 1987 and 1988, a subcommittee of the Senate Foreign Relations Committee, chaired by Senator John Kerry of Massachusetts, found direct links between international drug dealers based in the USA and the Contras, the violent extremist paramilitary group in Nicaragua supported by the U.S. government. The committee found evidence of Panamanian dictator Manuel Noriega's involvement in drug smuggling as well.

Kerry and his staff had videotaped depositions from Contra leaders who said they received drug profits to fund their group's operations with the knowledge of the CIA. Pilots who shipped the drugs admitted to flying weapons down to Nicaragua and taking cocaine and marijuana back to the US. In at least one instance, they landed their drug shipment at

Homestead Air Force Base in Florida. All this was comprehensively documented in U.S Customs reports, FBI reports, and Justice Department memos.

Back in the 1980s, before Gary Webb dug into the story in the 1990s, several reporters tried to cover it, and their careers and lives were ruined. Robert Parry and Brian Barger of the Associated Press covered the story, as did NYT freelancers Martha Honey and Tony Avirgan. The latter two were set up on phony drug charges, smeared, and ruined financially.

You will see time and time again that when any member of the press tries actually to hold power accountable in our system, they will be demonized, humiliated, dragged through the mud, and eventually imprisoned in a dark cell and held without trial (Julian Assange).

When Gary Webb tracked down a Contra supporter named Dennis Ainsworth, he was told the following,

"You've got to be crazy. Nobody in Washington wanted to look at this. They wanted this story buried, and anyone who looked any deeper into it got buried along with it. You're bringing up a very old nightmare. You have no idea what you are touching on here, Gary. No idea at all. I almost got killed. I had friends in Central America who were killed. There was a Mexican reporter who was looking into one end of this, and he wound up dead."

In Central America, a guy the U.S. government loved and supported for years was a dictatorial stooge named Anastasio Somoza, whose family had ruled the Republic of Nicaragua for 46 years. He had done everything the U.S. told him to do over the years. In fact, Somoza worked with the CIA during the Bay of Pigs fiasco. "The U.S. calls me, and I agreed to have the bombers leave here and knock the hell out of the installations in Cuba," Somoza said. In 1965, Somoza sent troops to support a U.S.-led invasion of the Dominican Republic to put down a people's uprising.

But Somoza had a problem: The Sandinistas, a leftist rebel group with popular support, did not like Somoza's heavy-handed, dictatorial, U.S.-aligned rule.

Unfortunately for Somoza, decades of corruption, crime, murder, and torture led to his people wanting him dead, so on July 17, 1979, Somoza and his top generals, business partners, and families were flown to Homestead Air Force Base to live in exile before a popular uprising took more than their wealth.

Once Somoza was exiled, others connected to him also fled to the U.S. to avoid prosecution by the Sandinistas. Once there, they began to set up the beginnings of the paramilitary terrorist organization known as The Contras, earlier known as the FDN, and before that, the **Legion of September 15**.

Even the CIA admitted the Contras/FDN/Legion weren't very nice people.

In 1998, the CIA said the Contras/Legion "to some extent engaged in kidnapping, extortion, and robbery to fund its operations" and also "engaged in the bombing of Nicaraguan civilian airlines and airliner hijacking as methods of attacking the Sandinista government."

Hmm, it seems the U.S. government is perfectly OK with supporting state-sponsored terrorism if they are on the right side.

One of the most public operations the Legion performed was the March 1980 assassination of the Roman Catholic archbishop of San Salvador, Oscar Romero, who was shot through the heart as he held Sunday Mass. Nice huh? Murdering a priest in front of his congregation during service. How would US Christians feel about that happening here? The CIA sure likes to cozy up to interesting groups. Eventually, the Legion was absorbed into a group the CIA manufactured, the Fuerza Democratica Nicaragiuense, also called the FDN, which would ultimately turn into the Contras.

As part of building their anti-Sandinista (aka anti-Communist) efforts, the CIA employed and worked with ruthless drug dealers like Norwin Meneses, a drug trafficker and killer who was referred to as *The Godfather*. A 1982 FBI report said Meneses "had a reputation as a hit man who had killed in Nicaragua." The CIA referred to him in 1986 as "the kingpin of narcotics traffickers in Nicaragua before the fall of Somoza."

In Nicaragua, there was a very powerful and corrupt organization that the CIA helped to build and fund, called **the Guardia**. One researcher called this organization "one of the most totally corrupt military establishments in the world." Yikes! The Guardia was closely connected to the success of the Meneses family.

The Guardia wasn't just an Army like we think of one. It was the CIA, FBI, DEA, IRS, Army, Air Force, Marines, National Guard, Coast Guard, Immigration, Customs, and Postal Service all rolled into one. That is how powerful and all-encompassing Somoza's Guardia was. To most people in Nicaragua, the Guardia was little more than a state-sponsored mafia group, with members of the Meneses family of drug dealers and killers as leaders.

"Gambling, alcoholism, drugs, prostitution, and other vices are protected and exploited by the very persons who have an obligation to combat them." - Nicaragua's Roman Catholic Bishops told Somoza in a 1978 letter.

Meneses, The Guardia, Somoza, and the CIA were all thick as thieves. An FBI informant told the Justice Department that Meneses used his influence with the Somoza regime to smuggle cocaine from Colombia to the U.S. and "even used a Nicaraguan Air Force plane once for such a shipment." Convenient. I wonder if they used U.S. Air Bases to land drugs. Yes, yes, they did. Norwin Meneses and his family are central players in the CIA's development of the Contra organization.

"Even before the term Contra was being used…there were meetings of anti-Sandinistas at Meneses' house, which were attended by politicians, Somoza followers, and other exiles interested in starting a counter-revolutionary movement," said a DEA informant to the Justice Department in 1997.

This huge international drug dealer and murderer, already identified as such by the US government as early as 1974, came and went as he pleased in and out of the USA with little to no government oversight. By 1986, Meneses was bragging that he had US government agents escorting him across America's borders. This was, in fact, the truth.

All while US law enforcement was well aware of Meneses' criminal activities. In 1978, the FBI knew Norwin Meneses and his brother Ernest were smuggling 20 kilos of cocaine at a time into the United States." The DEA knew this, too. "The Drug Enforcement Administration has developed information over the past several years that the Meneses Family has been involved in the smuggling and distribution of cocaine in the San Francisco Bay Area," according to a DEA agent in 1981. According to another insider, the Meneses organization moved almost a ton of cocaine into the USA in 1981, about $54 million at wholesale. These were no small players.

Meneses and his cronies were working directly with CIA agents who encouraged and supported them in finding ways to raise money to establish the Contras against the Sandinistas. CIA agent Enrique Bermudez told them to raise funds for the counter-revolution; however, they needed to. There was simply no other way to generate this level of funding without illegal drugs. Starting to make more sense why drugs are still prohibited? How could illegal off-the-books military operations be funded without illicit drug money? They couldn't.

In Sept. 1981, the CIA was informed by a cable that Contras' "leadership has made a decision to engage in drug smuggling to the USA in order to finance its anti-Sandinista operations." The CIA did not attempt to halt these activities.

THE USA's position on Nicaragua and Central America shifted radically when Ronald Reagan and George Bush (ex-CIA director) took office. They, unlike the Carter administration, were firmly against the popular uprising of the Sandinistas and wanted to support the murdering, torturing, drug-dealing ex-Somoza thugs, who would become the Contras. Within days of taking office, Reagan froze all aid to the Sandinista government.

In 1981, the CIA began a more formal undermining of the Sandinista government by funding and supplying anti-Sandinista groups in the USA. Outside of Miami, Cuban Bay of Pigs veterans put up training camps for the Contras and even had the US press come to see them being trained by former Green Berets. Other Contra training camps were set up in California and Texas. Then the CIA began uniting the various ex-Somoza groups in the USA under one umbrella organization.

At the time, the CIA's role in creating and organizing those who would eventually become the Contras was hidden. But it was made public in 1985 when former FDN director Edgar Chamorro filed an affidavit with the World Court in The Hague. In it, he revealed,

"The name of the operation, the members of the political junta, and the members of the general staff were all chosen or approved by the CIA."

The CIA was very proud of its revolutionary group of thugs, so in November 1981, they moved to make the organization official. Ronald Reagan was presented with a document known as National Security Decision Directive #17, which was a blueprint for the US government's plan to overthrow the

Sandinista government. The directive called for the CIA to conduct covert operations, both military and political, against the Sandinistas and asked for $19.95 million to do it. They made it clear this was just the starting bill, as "more funds and manpower" would be needed later.

How exciting, huh? This process is precisely how the USA intervenes in countries that do not play ball with us or our corporations and owner class, and how they set up and incite revolutions by extremist elements against legitimate governments. This process continues to this day in places like Ukraine.

From 1981 to 1984, the CIA ran the Contra operation directly, giving out weapons and money, hiring subcontractors, ferrying supplies, planning strategy and tactics, and keeping tabs on everyone. The Nicaraguans were expected to follow orders and fight, while the American CIA advisers directed them from up high. All Contra supporters were told to deny any connection to the CIA. Former FDN director Edgar Chamorro said CIA advisers prepped Contra leaders and supporters for news conferences and told them to deny getting money from the US.

"It was particularly important that we deny having met with any US government officials."

Why is the US government embarrassed by its support of the Contras? If they were legitimate freedom fighters like the Reagan administration advertised, we should be proud of our support, no?

All the while, illegal drug money by ex-Somoza drug dealers was funding some of the operations and support for the FDN/Contras. In fact, they were getting their coke directly from the infamous Cali cartel. You've heard of them.

What was great for these Contra drug dealers was that anytime they got caught by the FBI, DEA, or local police, they would walk away with a slap on the wrist once their handlers from US intelligence got involved. One major international cocaine trafficker, Horacio Pereira, only had to pay a small fine for smuggling $70,000 in cash from cocaine sales. He was sent back to Costa Rica with no probation and no prison. He just continued his drug dealing from there.

Let's all keep in mind that at the time during the 80s, Ronald Reagan was a big anti-drug, no-tolerance, moral crusader kind of guy. Hysterical.

This conflict of interest between CIA-sponsored Contra drug dealers and federal agents or police persecuting drug dealers was first publicly exposed on January 17, 1983. On this day, FBI agents arrested several men who were smuggling 430 pounds of cocaine out of the San Francisco Bay, worth a street value of $100 million. This was a big bust as it was the first by Ronald Reagan's new federal Drug Task Force. But there was bad news too, as they busted one of the CIA's prime pets, Norwin Meneses, who was smuggling the coke.

You may think there would be hell to pay for such a big bust of poison for our kids, but luckily, our Nicaraguan heroes walked scot-free and were not prosecuted. Norwin Meneses had a DEA agent on his payroll, so he was warned early and distanced himself from the deal.

Even better, when this case did come to court, like many others that would follow it, the CIA would get involved to seal information and hide phone records to conceal the government's collusion and partnership with these drug smugglers. In the end, some low-level guys got busted, but the big ones never did. That is, until the big ones were no longer of use to the US politically, then they could be taken down and made an example of.

"We only capture a drug lord when he is no longer a drug lord." – Alfred McCoy.

IN the early 80s, the Reagan administration was all hopped up on **anti-Communism** in Central America, or so it claimed. This continued a 30-year tradition of Communist/leftist paranoia and ideological governance that has consumed American society post-WW2, initially driven by the Dulles brothers' power-circle partnership from the 50s to the 70s.

In reality, the Reagan admin was concerned with U.S. hegemony in the western hemisphere and the control the US maintained over other countries to benefit our multinational corporations and ruling class. But they liked to call it anti-Communist because that means freedom and democracy, or something like that. Anti-communism is and was as much about power and control as the drug war is. It's a tool and a propaganda framework to use to justify criminal and immoral activities, jockeying for power and control by elitist elements.

So, at the time, one of the Reagan administration's doctrines was to keep leftists out of power in El Salvador since they had taken over in Nicaragua. The CIA used this excuse to ramp up their full-scale, covert war against the Sandinistas in Nicaragua, claiming that this legitimate government was, in fact, evil Communists.

In neighboring El Salvador, a similar process was playing out, as seen in Nicaragua. To try to control the popular uprising against brutal US-backed authoritarianism, the government unleashed terrorist death squads to roam around the countryside and kidnap suspected troublemakers, and torture and murder them.

"Under the guise of anti-Communism, the death squads terrorized the entire country – murdering nuns, teachers, labor organizers, political opponents, and thousands of other civilians," - Lieutenant Colonel Oliver North, Under Fire.

One El Salvadoran official who committed the worst atrocities was a $ 90,000-a-year CIA-paid asset, Colonel Nicholas Carranza, head of the government's Treasury Police. This guy was such a scumbag that CIA director William Casey met with Carranza personally in the summer of 1983 to tell him to "knock it off," or the CIA would kick him off the payroll. The CIA sure seems to have lots of very awful people on its payroll.

Things were going just fine when, in October 1984, the CIA and their Contras got caught putting anti-ship mines in Nicaraguan harbors, damaging international shipping, US allies included. Oops! After this incident, all CIA funding for the Contras was cut off by Congress. Double Oops! More on that later.

A lawyer for Danilo Blandon, a top Norwin Meneses drug dealer in the U.S., said the following about how the Contras made their money after funding was cut: "The Contras…had no above-the-line funding. Everything was sub rosa, and one of the ways they were trying to make money was importing cocaine."

The Nicaraguan and Colombian drug lords, smugglers, and dealers had lots of help from law enforcement, and not just seeing their cases dismissed in court. They had direct help from guys like Ronald Jay Lister. Lister had been a police officer near LA and a military police officer as well. He was a detective in the burglary division of the Laguna Beach Police Department. Eventually, he became an employee working for Danilo Blandon, the Contra drug dealer.

His former CIA chief, Neil Purcell, remembers Lister well. "The man, in my opinion, is a lying, conniving, manipulative person who likes to play with people's minds. He's very evasive and loves living on the edge. He's the biggest bullshitter that has ever been placed on this earth."

Just the right kind of cop to work with violent cocaine drug lords and the CIA.

Between 1983 and 1986, the FBI opened five separate investigations of Lister, all for trafficking illegal weapons and high-tech equipment to foreign governments. Lister and Blandon's front company, Pyramid International, was being investigated by the FBI for "the sale of weapons to El Salvador and the loan of money from Saudi Arabia to the Salvadoran government." Arms maker Timothy LaFrance, who worked with Lister, described Pyramid International as "a private vendor that the CIA used to do things (the agency) couldn't do."

Considering that at the time the Saudi government was helping to finance covert operations for the Reagan administration, the fact that the FBI dropped the probe into Lister and Pyramid International may seem conspicuous. The reality was the El Salvador operation was all being done so the CIA could arm and support the Contras to invade Nicaragua.

The Pyramid team eventually moved into a military-run mass transit center in downtown San Salvador. According to LaFrance, "That's where we made weapons." After the finished guns were transported to a Salvadoran military airstrip in Morazán province, they were then airlifted to Contra camps in Honduras.

In 1983, LaFrance said he was hired by the Cabazon Indian tribe in southern California to build an arms factory on their tiny, desolate land. It turns out that the tribal administrators worked for the CIA, and he and Wackenhut International Inc., a security firm that the S.F. Chronicle described as being "led by former officials of the CIA, the FBI, NSA, Defense

Department, and federal law enforcement," were making weapons for the Contras there.

This is when reporters started dying. Freelance investigative reporter Danny Casolaro was looking into all of this as part of a conspiracy investigation when he was found dead in a West Virginia motel room in 1991, supposedly from a suicide. He has told friends that,

"Spies, arms merchants, and others were using an Indian reservation as a low-profile site on which to develop weapons for Third World armies, including the Nicaraguan Contras."

TERRY Reid is a former Air Force intelligence officer and FBI informant who became involved in the CIA Contra project in the mid-80s. In his memoirs called *Compromised*, Reed stated that he scouted locations and provided a corporate shell for CIA agents working with the Contras in Mexico from 1985 to 1986, in part to keep the supply of weapons flowing when Congress cut off the CIA's funding of the Contras. Reid said that CIA operatives were shipping cocaine through the company he helped set up in Mexico.

One of the people Reid worked with at the time was Adler Berriman Seal, a CIA and DEA contract agent and a pilot who ran drugs and weapons out of Mena, Arkansas, Intermountain Regional Airport. In the early 80s, Barry Seal was one of the biggest cocaine and marijuana smugglers in the U.S., flying loads of drugs into the USA from the Medellin cartel and air-dropping them into the southern U.S. A letter from Louisiana's attorney general to U.S. Attorney General Ed Meese said Seal "smuggled between $3 billion and $5 billion worth of drugs into the U.S." This guy was no small potatoes.

According to a 1983 U.S. Customs report, Seal's farm in Baton Rouge was used as a drop site for cocaine and marijuana shipments. The same plane that Seal used to smuggle drugs was found flying supplies for the Contras in 1985 and was discovered to be owned by a family member of a Contra leader.

Oh, did I forget to tell you that Seal was also an informant for the DEA, who worked with the CIA-DEA in sting operations trying to set up Sandinista government officials in drug smuggling? Remember Oliver North? Well, according to Congressional records, he was being briefed regularly by the CIA on Seal's sting operation. I wonder why?

On February 17, 1986, Seal was murdered in New Orleans by Colombian hitmen. Seal's "personal records showed him to be a contract CIA operative both before and during his years of drug-running in Mena in the 1980s," historian Roger Morris wrote in his book Partners in Power, about Bill and Hillary Clinton.

Four months after his assassination, Oliver North called the FBI and claimed there was an "active measures program" being directed against him by the Sandinistas. North claimed people were following him and directing death threats and smears against him. An FBI agent wrote,

"North expressed further concern that he may be targeted for elimination by organized crime due to his alleged involvement in drug running."

So, here is Oliver North admitting to the FBI on record that he is involved in international drug smuggling.

After a Senate subcommittee looked into the whole issue, including the connection to the Contras, the investigation was dropped due to concerns about revealing national security information.

The big question here is, did Bill Clinton know about this drug smuggling while he was Governor of Arkansas? Could this number of drugs and weapons be flown in and out of Arkansas without the Governor knowing? Larry Patterson, a former Arkansas state trooper and security for Clinton, said,

"That there were large quantities of drugs being flown into the Mena airport, large quantities of money, large quantities of guns. That there were ongoing operations training foreign people in that area. That it was a CIA operation."

A mechanic at Mena airport, John Bender, swore in a deposition that he saw Clinton there three times in 1985. Trooper L.D. Brown said he confronted Governor Clinton about Seal's smuggling flights, when Clinton replied, "That's Lasater's deal."

Little Rock bond broker Danny Ray Lasater was a close friend and donor to Clinton. In 1986, Lasater was indicted by a federal grand jury in Little Rock on drug charges, and Clinton's brother, Roger, a cocaine addict, was named an unindicted coconspirator. Lasater pleaded guilty to drug trafficking, served six months, and was pardoned by Clinton in 1990.

All of this apparently was some crazy conspiracy theory, right? A Clinton spokesman called the reports of Clinton's knowledge of the Mena operation "the darkest backwater of the right-wing conspiracy theory industry."

Not too ironically, the plane that Seal was using to smuggle drugs and guns from and to the U.S. was shot down over Nicaragua in 1985 with a SAM missile, breaking the whole Iran-Contra scandal wide open.

But let's not forget about the big players here, namely one of the largest drug lords in the western hemisphere, named Norwin Meneses. His own involvement in the Contra gun-running operation was confirmed in 1996 by the New York Times, which quoted an unnamed Clinton administration official saying that Meneses had "contacts with the Contras in Honduras in 1982 or 1983 or 1984 and that he was believed then to have had some involvement in arms smuggling as well as money laundering and drugs."

HAPPENING parallel to all this government-sponsored criminal drug dealing and arms smuggling, in LA, a young man was making a name for himself in the local drug business named Ricky Ross. Ricky was from South Central and would grow to be one of the biggest cocaine/crack dealers on the West Coast. He started dealing cocaine in small amounts, but then heard about crack and freebase cocaine, which were getting popular, so he switched to being primarily a rock cocaine dealer. Making rock cocaine is pretty straightforward. You put the coke powder in a pan, add water and baking soda, and heat until it starts crackling. And bam, you got crack!

In the early 80s, crack was beginning to take off in America. It was easy to use, addictive, and cheap, at least compared to powder cocaine, which was more popular with richer white people. Just as crack was getting popular in South Central, in part due to the vast amounts being brought in by the CIA/Meneses operation to support the Contras, it was also taking off in Miami. In Miami, it was Jamaican drug gangs that were in charge, not Colombians or Nicaraguans. But they started the same way the Nicaraguans did because they were also political exiles connected to similar US/CIA operations in Central America and the Caribbean.

Let's see how our ever-present dungeon master, the CIA, connects these events.

Since the 1970s, Jamaica has been run by a socialist government led by Michael Manley, a graduate of the London School of Economics. Soon after taking power, Manley pissed off the U.S. by recognizing the Cuban government of Fidel Castro and supporting socialist rebels that a CIA proxy army was fighting in Angola. This is a no-no since, as we all know, the US only likes regimes that play ball.

In 1977, two investigative reports uncovered a "destabilization program" against Manley's government being run by the CIA Jamaican station chief, Norman Descoteaux. The program consisted of the covert shipment of arms to Manley's opponents, the use of violence, bombings, and assassinations, covert financial aid of the conservative party in Jamaica, the instigation of labor unrest, and bribery. CIA agents who are known to be involved with the Contras were present in at least one bombing in Jamaica.

This is what the CIA does on the world stage, right up until today, they are doing the same thing, God knows where else. But let's get back to Ricky again.

The way Ricky got his supply after he started turning big was from one of Norwin Meneses' main drug men, Danielo Blandon. I mentioned him a bit earlier, remember? You'll see that everyone in this story works very closely together and crisscrosses relationships and contacts. It turns out Danielo Blandon was the biggest Nicaraguan cocaine dealer in the USA. And his boss was protected from up high at the CIA.

Ricky got really big, really fast by selling crack in volume and at scale, selling between 1,000,000 and 1,250,000 rocks every month.

"There is no doubt that Ricky Ross created a massive distribution network that poured enormous amounts of crack into Los Angeles, and elsewhere, during the mid-1980s." - the Justice Department's Inspector General, 1998

ABOUT a year after the CIA took over financing the Contras, Newsweek magazine published an account of the Reagan administration's support of the Contras titled "America's Secret War: Target Nicaragua." According to one account, the source for the Newsweek story was CIA Director William Casey, who was trying to ensure the Contra project continued and wanted to shore up support. This continued a long history of US intelligence feeding misinformation to the friendly press to create narratives it wants support for, like manufacturing wars. And the US press is a willing dupe and compatriot in this exchange.

After the Newsweek story came out, some congressmen wanted a funding cutoff for the Contras, since they were a known group of murderers, rapists, terrorists, and criminals. In fact, one senator called them "vicious, cutthroat murderers." In response, the House passed on Christmas Eve, 1982, by 411-0 votes an amendment that prohibited the use of taxpayer dollars "for the purpose of overthrowing the government of Nicaragua or provoking a military exchange between Nicaragua and Honduras."

But as is the case with most supposed laws to rein in unchecked power, it had no teeth and was designed to make it look like Congress was cracking down on the Contra project without actually doing anything. If you read my book *The Money to Control*, you will see time and time again that the impetus of reform is, in fact, used to further the abuse of power.

And just like the Pentagon Papers revealed the truth about the impossibility of winning the US war in Vietnam, internal government memos show that the CIA, White House, and the Defense Department all knew the Contras had no chance of defeating the Sandinistas. None of this mattered; the money kept flowing into the Contras in ever-increasing amounts.

In fact, according to the journalist Sam Dillon, the CIA was sending "tens of thousands of dollars a month to the general staff (an FDN leader)" in which his "staff officers were pocketing the money. They were also stealing half the CIA food budget."

Does this remind anyone of the billions of dollars our government has sent to Zelenskyy and Ukraine, in which at least 50% of it is being stolen and misdirected to the black market?

Now, let's not forget that while the CIA is sending US citizens taxpayer money directly to a group of terrorists, at the same time, Blandon and Meneses are also selling cocaine to American citizens to fund the Contras. Blandon said in a grand jury testimony,

"In 1983, the Contras got a lot of money from the United States. And when Reagan gets in power, we start receiving a lot of money. And the people that were in charge, the CIA, so they didn't want to raise any money, they had all the money they wanted."

According to an August 1986 DEA report, "The principal group is controlled by Blandon and is the focal point for drug supply and money laundering for the others. The other group, run by Meneses, is located in the San Francisco area. Cocaine is transported to the Blandon association and then from Blandon to Meneses in San Francisco."

"Oh, he (Meneses) was totally protected by the U.S. government," said Contra supporter Dennis

Ainsworth. "He was protected by everyone under the sun."

Huh. No wonder cocaine and crack were so readily available in the 80s in the USA. It was being imported on an industrial scale by a guy working for the US government and the CIA. Charming.

To make all this happen, then, just like now, the CIA is running psychological ops (psyops) campaigns against the American public and others to convince people the Contras were good, and the Sandinistas were bad.

"Senior CIA officials with backgrounds in covert operations, as well as military intelligence and psychological operations specialists from the Department of Defense, were deeply involved in establishing and participating in a domestic political and propaganda operation run through an obscure bureau in the Department of State," a 1992 House committee staff report found. "Almost all of these activities were hidden from public view, and many of the individuals involved were never questioned or interviewed by the Iran/Contra committees."

Through that office, the CIA and the National Security Council engaged in "a domestic, covert operation designed to lobby the Congress, manipulate the media and influence domestic public opinion," the report said, supporting another 1987 investigation by the Comptroller General of the United States, which said the State Department had engaged in "prohibited, covert propaganda activities."

An informant said he received cash directly from Oliver North, and CIA agent Adolfo Calero, between 1986 and 1987, "to affect public opinion favorably towards the Reagan positions inside, regarding Central America."

Has anything changed today? If anything, this is much worse than before and has all been normalized. There are no more Congressional investigations. Hush-hush.

How much did the CIA and the US government know about Contras and Meneses' drug smuggling? According to one informant, "The CIA knows about all these things…The money for the Contras received from the Reagan Administration was peanuts, and the growing military organization needed supplies, arms, food, and money to support the families of the Contras. The CIA decided to recruit Meneses so that drug sales could be used to support the Contras."

The problem was that this whole thing was getting out of control; the drug business and crack were growing so fast, and they were making so much money that drug dealing became the primary goal.

An informant said the FDN/Contras "has become more involved in selling arms and cocaine for personal gain than in a military effort to overthrow the current Nicaraguan Sandinista government."

THINGS started getting really bad for the Contras and their CIA handlers by the mid-80s due to a series of blunders by the ever-blundering CIA. In the spring of 1984, the CIA planted hundreds of mines in Nicaraguan harbors, which then started blowing holes in cargo ships from around the world, including allies of the USA. Then later in the year, an illustrated how-to-be-a-terrorist manual that the CIA printed up for their employees in the field was made public, causing more uncomfortable focus on the CIA Contra project.

Then, in 1984, Congress passed a resolution that prohibited the CIA, the Defense Department, or any other US agency from giving money or aid to anyone for the support of the Contras. After this, the CIA and Defense Department began withdrawing their trainers, advisers, administrators, tacticians, and logicians from Central America.

In 1985, news of the Contra crimes started to become more public, coming from human rights groups, which highlighted murders, tortures, assassinations, and the use of terror by Contra field commanders. This is all very disconnected from Reagan's pitch for the Contras, in which he compared them to the Founding Fathers of the American Revolution. Hmm. Maybe Reagan was a bit off base. Please read my other two books to get an idea of the types of people the Founding Fathers were and what their motives were.

During all this, Nicaraguans Blandon and Meneses, who sold cocaine in the USA to fund the Contras, found their businesses getting bigger and bigger, as they helped fuel the crack cocaine explosion. And they didn't just supply LA-based drug gangs with dope, they also sold them assault rifles, submachine guns, advanced communications, and eavesdropping gear. Ah, now we know how all those gangs got armed with such serious weapons, from the CIA's own employees.

During all this bad press and *just say no* drug war from Nancy Reagan, one of the biggest drug dealers in the USA, Danielo Blandon, was given approval from the State Department for political asylum and made an official guest of the US government. Now, keep in mind that the DEA, CIA, and everyone in the government know this guy is one of the largest drug dealers in the US, so why are they giving him asylum? A State Department official said there was a blanket zero-tolerance policy for immigrant narcotics suspects. And don't forget this guy, who was just given asylum in the US, is the leading supplier for the largest crack dealer in LA, Ricky Ross. Ricky, in the mid-80s, was selling 3,000,000 doses of crack every seven days in LA.

According to the US General Accounting Office (GAO) in a 1989 report, "In the early 1980s, the gangs began selling crack cocaine. Within a matter of years, the lucrative crack market changed the black gangs from traditional neighborhood street gangs to extremely violent criminal groups operating from coast to coast. Within the past 3-4 years, members of the Crips and the Bloods have been identified selling or distributing crack in Washington, Oregon, Kansas, Oklahoma, Colorado, Missouri, North Carolina, Arizona, Virginia, Maryland, and elsewhere."

All of this was happening on a national/international industrial scale. A commission that examined the causes of the 1992 riots in South Central named crack as one of the contributing factors. Well, along with abject poverty, racial discrimination, wage slavery, police brutality, plus a host of other mitigating factors.

Not only did Nicaraguan drug dealers like Blandon and Meneses sell drugs in high volume to black street gangs, but they also sold them all the guns and advanced weaponry, too. All thanks to that wonderful ex-cop named Ronald J. Lister. According to Ross, Blandon… "started selling us guns after that. Everybody who worked for me, everybody, bought a gun from him." According to Blandon, the guns he sold to crack dealers came from Ronald Lister through his security businesses in Laguna Beach. That business was Mundy Security Group Inc.

Blandon didn't just sell crack dealers, coke, and guns; he also sold them high-end electronic surveillance equipment. He sold walkie-talkies, pagers, police scanners, voice scramblers, cellular phones, and anti-eavesdropping devices. All procured from Ronald Lister, that shining light of law enforcement.

But when investigators tried to look into Lister's background when he was accused of selling equipment to KGB agents, they found that "the City of Maywood has sealed the personnel jacket for Ronald J. Lister." Also, in the Laguna Beach Police Department, they found that "the actual personnel files related to Ronald Lister no longer existed." Convenient huh?

It becomes less surprising when you see the types of friends and associates Mr. Lester had. One was Bill Nelson, former CIA deputy director of operations, in charge of all CIA covert activity from 1973 to 1976, and a protégé of CIA director William Colby. As head of covert operations, Nelson oversaw the CIA destabilization program in Chile, which resulted in the overthrow and murder of Chile's democratically elected president, Salvador Allende.

When you look at Nelson's operation in Chile, it resembles the one in Nicaragua, and dozens of others since. In these operations, arms and equipment for the CIA's secret armies were laundered through the armies of neighboring countries friendly to the US to disguise their origins and to provide plausible deniability for the CIA. In both operations, the CIA got additional weapons and missiles from the People's Republic of China. Wait a second? Isn't this all about the halting of the Communist creep? Containment? So why is the CIA buying weapons from a Communist country to give to terrorist goons in Central America to overthrow a democratically elected group of leftists? Strange bedfellows indeed.

Oh, it gets murkier for the CIA. A CIA operative in Mexico, Lawrence Victor Harrison, testified that the CIA was collaborating with the Mexican intelligence service and drug cartel bosses who were providing money, arms, and training facilities for the Contras in exchange for the CIA's protection of their drug empires.

So, let's get this straight. Not only did the CIA turn the other way and provide cover and protection for Nicaraguan drug dealers in the USA, but it also acted as a mafioso enforcer to protect drug gangs for their support of the Contra effort. Wow. These are facts, people, not theories.

Once Congress pulled funding for the Contra, go-getters like Oliver North came in and, with the assistance of lawyers and CIA Director William Casey, created a network of offshore bank accounts to conceal the source of money for the Contra to hide from Congress.

The reality is the CIA couldn't have cared less about drugs being brought into the USA by Nicaraguans; all they cared about was trying to pin drug trafficking on the Sandinista government.

"All of the Central American Stations were seeing information that would link the Sandinistas to drug trafficking," a top CIA official told the Inspector

General. "The goal was to diminish the image of the Sandinistas."

And the CIA was perfectly happy to work with Contra drug dealers to accomplish their goals. According to a CIA station chief, "we were going to play with these guys. That was made clear by (CIA Director) Casey."

Oh, don't forget about one of the largest international drug dealers in the world, Norwin Meneses. In a 1988 cable to FBI HQ, an FBI agent said, "It became apparent to the FBI that Norwin Meneses was, and may still be, an informant of the DEA. It is also believed by the FBI that Norwin Meneses was, and may still be, an informant for the CIA." Wow. One of the largest cocaine dealers in the world, the man who helped fuel the entire 1980s crack craze in the USA, is protected up high by the DEA and CIA.

ALL of this was not happening in a vacuum. What the Contras built in Costa Rica in the mid-80s, according to a special Costa Rican legislative commission, served as an HQ for an "organization made up of Panamanians, Colombians, Costa Ricans, and citizens of other nationalities who dedicated themselves to international cocaine trafficking, using Costa Rica as a bridge for the refueling of planes that came from Colombia." This drug ring was being run by the Contras with the assistance of Panamanian dictator General Manuel Noriega, according to the commission.

Evidence from a DEA investigation of Manuel Noriega found his drug trafficking ring loaded planes with cocaine in Colombia, refueled at Contra airstrips in northern Costa Rica, before going to the USA and offloading in Louisiana and Texas. But even with so much evidence and apparent criminality, the USA, for some reason, couldn't or didn't do anything about it.

"Despite obvious and widespread trafficking through the war zones of Northern Costa Rica, the Subcommittee was unable to find a single case against a drug trafficker operating in these zones which was made on the basis of a tip or report by an official of a U.S. intelligence agency," a US subcommittee reported in 1988. "This is despite an executive order requiring intelligence agencies to report trafficking to law enforcement officials."

Jorge Chavarria, a prosecutor for Costa Rica, said he was convinced the DEA "knew about the Contras and drugs. All these flights and pilots that were flying in and out with drugs could not have been ignored by the DEA. They were looking in the other direction."

EVERYTHING came to a head with the Contras and the CIA in 1985. In Costa Rica, there was a famous revolutionary doctor of the middle class, Dr. Hugo Spadafora. In September, his body was found tortured and dead on the border of Costa Rica and Panama. It turns out that this doctor was about to blow the whistle on General Manuel Noriega, the dictator of Panama, for being an international drug smuggler, who, as we mentioned before, was working directly with the Contras, and was protected by the CIA, to smuggle cocaine into the US. Noriega himself ordered Dr. Spadafora tortured and killed.

After this happened, a New York Times story in June 1986 said,

"Officials in the Reagan Administration and past Administrations said in interviews that they had overlooked General Noriega's illegal activities because of his cooperation with American intelligence. They said, for example, General Noriega had been a valuable asset to Washington in countering insurgencies in Central America and was now cooperating with the CIA in providing sensitive information from Nicaragua."

A month after Dr. Spadafora's torture and murder, Noriega's underlings contacted their friends in the CIA. They asked for help in "defusing an effort by family members of slain rebel Hugo Spadafora to implicate Manuel Antonio Noriega in drug trafficking."

Strangely enough, the CIA and US government were not crazy about letting people know that they had international drug traffickers like Noriega on their payroll, so the investigation into the murder was quickly buried. Even more important, Noriega was key to the government's plans with the Contras, and he was meeting with Oliver North, now head of the Contra program, to discuss how he could help.

According to Blandon, a convicted drug smuggler, "Colonel North was interested in gaining Panama's support for the Contras, and he particularly requested training assistance in bases located in Panama," he testified to Congress in 1988. "General Noriega promised to provide training in specific locations to members of the Contras, training to be provided at bases located in Panama."

Within one year, as payment for his assistance to the Contras, Panama's U.S.-funded foreign aid increased by $200 million.

All the while, US intelligence supports and protects Noriega in his own international drug smuggling operation as long as he agrees to help with the Contras. According to a Senate Subcommittee report, CIA Director William Casey said he decided not to address allegations of Noriega's cocaine trafficking "on the ground that Noriega was providing valuable support for our policies in Central America."

Oliver North at this point was the leading man when it came to the Contras. Since the US had pulled the plug on official Contra support, North was making new logistics to fund and supply them. He had to plan air supply, weapons, food, etc., for an entire 15,000-man army in the field, all in secret. North did some of this by claiming the money was going to humanitarian causes in Nicaragua.

Another nice way they got money to the Contras was by laundering cocaine cartel money. The Medellin cartel's accountant, Ramon Milian Rodriguez, testified to Congress that he used a shrimp company called Frigorificos de

Puntarenas to launder a $10 million donation from the Medellin cartel to the Contras, a donation he said was arranged by and paid to a former CIA agent.

These front companies, or cutouts, are how the CIA operates and runs black ops like the Contra affair. A former drug smuggling pilot testified that the Frigorificos shrimp company was being used by the Contras during the war as a front to bring cocaine into the US to finance the war effort. This particular front company got a contract with the Nicaraguan Humanitarian Assistance Program, thanks to the CIA, the records show. In fact, the Costa Rican manager of this company was a CIA agent.

This is all one big happy family, isn't it? In fact, the CIA protected the drug dealers it was working with. At the same time, the CIA's Directorate of Operations, which runs its covert ops, lied to the CIA's lawyers, denying knowledge of the shrimp company. However, there was plenty of evidence on file.

All of these facts came out in court during Manuel Noriega's trial for drug trafficking. An informant testified that he was flying weapons to the Contras and flying coke into the US, and a lawyer asked whether Oliver North knew about this. The Judge became visibly angry and immediately shut down the line of questioning. "Just stay away from it." He would not allow any more questions on the topic.

This is how you use the judicial system to hide government secrets and crimes, through their stooges in the courts, elitist judges.

At this point, North had gotten things back up and running quite nicely after Congress pulled official funding for the Contras. According to Blandon's lawyer, "As I understood it, these large transports were coming back from delivering food and guns and humanitarian aid and things like that, and they were just loading them up with cocaine and bringing them back. I think 1,000-kilo shipments were not unheard of."

Oliver North and the CIA had set up a base for drug and gun smuggling in El Salvador at the Ilopango Air Force Base. A DEA agent who was stationed there was told not to investigate shady dealings too deeply. In fact, the Contra air supply operation was being run out in the open at the base. Day-to-day operations were being run by a CIA agent named Felix Rodrigues, a Bay of Pigs veteran and a paramilitary specialist.

The drugs that were coming into Ilopanga Air Force Base in El Salvador arrived in private planes flown by Contra pilots from Costa Rica. On other occasions, they would come in military aircraft from Panama. Anytime pilots were caught with money or drugs, the investigations were suddenly halted without explanation. When Freedom of Information Act (FOIA) requests were filed, the files were claimed to be lost. CIA records themselves show that the Agency used Hangars in El Salvador.

Once planes arrived in El Salvador, cocaine would be loaded onto US-bound aircraft owned by the Salvadorian Air Force or CIA-contractor Southern Air Transport. US military hardware, meanwhile, was flown south on Salvadoran transport planes, traded for cocaine, and flown back to Ilopango. During the 1980s, the US Justice Department received at least three reliable reports that detailed arms-for-drugs swaps involving the Medellin cartel, the Contras, and elements of the US government.

Oh, and according to a high-level informant, the Medellin cartel had made a deal with VP George Bush to supply American weapons to the Contras in exchange for free passage for their cocaine delivered to the US. This informant met with Pablo Escobar. He said Escobar described,

"An agreement or relationship between Bush and the American government and members of the Medellin cartel, which resulted in planes flying guns to the cartel in Colombia. Escobar stated that the cartel then offloaded the guns, put cocaine aboard the planes, and the cocaine was taken to US military bases. The guns were delivered and sold to the Contras in Nicaragua by the Cartel."

The informant also said Pablo Escobar claimed he had a picture of George Bush posing with the Medellin cartel leader, Jorge Ochoa, in front of suitcases full of money, and he was holding it to use as blackmail if needed. After Escobar was killed in 1993, the photo was never seen again.

See, it's all one big happy family. The CIA, terrorists, drug smugglers, the executive branch, the US Congress, and the El Salvadorian government are all in on it together, smuggling drugs, weapons, and money. According to an emissary for a Colombian cartel, "Norwin Meneses was selling drugs and funneling the benefits to the Contras with the help of high-ranking military officials of the Salvadoran Army." Oh, and in response to another FOIA request filed in 1997, the US Air Force said that all flight records of Salvadoran military aircraft from the mid-1980s were destroyed years ago. Convenient huh?

Meanwhile, the Reagan administration was hell-bent on blaming the Sandinistas for drug smuggling, but there was simply no evidence to support it. So, they leaked stories to the *Washington Times* falsely linking the Sandinistas to drug trafficking right before a critical Contra aid vote. These stories exposed the DEA's drug sting against the Medellin cartel, and the operation was ruined.

But don't worry, any and all concerns about guns-for-drugs deals between the Reagan administration and the Medellin cartel were conveniently never investigated. According to the Associate AG, "no action is being taken." Investigating DEA agents were told to "stop the witch hunt." In fact, a key DEA agent who was investigating this now found himself under investigation by the DEA itself, with claims he engaged in inappropriate activities and behaviors.

IN May 1986, a variety of corporate media outlets, including NBC, People, and the AP, ran stories on a deadly new drug that was supposedly destroying America, **CRACK**. It was the AP who said, "crack is becoming the nation's drug of choice." Really? The New York Times said "a wave of crack addicts" was spreading "prostitution and other crimes" across the nation. But was this true? Was there any data or evidence to back up these wild mainstream media assertions about crack?

Mainstream media's role, as discussed in my other books, is not to inform or enlighten the public, but to shift their opinion and consent to desirable ones that the owner class manufactures for them. According to drug researchers Andrew Golub and Donna Hartman,

"The U.S media followed a typical pattern in which exaggerated claims were supported by carefully selected cases and fueled with evocative words such as 'epidemic,' with its implications of plague, disease, crisis, and uncontrollable spread."

And according to all those brilliant media outlets, politicians, and law enforcement officers, the crack epidemic just happened, and no one knew how or why. Following these spectacular accusations by the press, there were two well-publicized congressional hearings in which government drug experts and officers expressed their dismay and shock about crack.

Representative Benjamin Gilman of New York asked this during a hearing. "Well, of course, you are telling us that crack is just beginning to spread across the country like wildfire in the past year. We have no current data, is that correct?" He asked a government expert.

"I think it would be fair to say that we do not have any accurate estimates at this time," replied Dr. Jerome Jaffe of the NIDA.

Huh. That's weird. Why are they all making these catastrophic statements on crack with zero data to support them? Maybe they all knew that something was driving the crack craze, and they didn't need to see the data to understand the results of their efforts. It was through the CIA, the Contras, and the Medellin cartel that cocaine was coming into the US and being made into crack in LA, at an industrial scale, all while being sanctioned and protected by the US government itself.

The reality is that the federal government had been warned about crack for years and did nothing to stop it, kind of like how they handled the SARS-CoV-2 pandemic, at least in regards to poor minorities. Dr. Robert Byck, Yale's top cocaine expert, said the following at a hearing.

"In 1979, I testified before the House Committee on Narcotics Abuse and Control, and I said that we were about to have the worst epidemic of drug use this country has ever seen, something like the speed epidemic of the 1960s, except on a national scale. I begged people. This advice went unheeded. Today we are in the midst of the predicted epidemic."

What was the solution? Surely not the preventative and supportive measures drug experts were proposing, which involved treatment and education. The solution would be more jails and more cops; somehow, that would solve our problem, which is based on zero data. It seems like this was the goal all along. To manufacture consent for public drug policy so it can be used to further the development of a national police state infrastructure, reducing civil liberties at home, and establishing the US as an international drug police force.

So, instead of authorizing money for crack research and educational campaigns, Congress voted for stricter laws for crack dealing. Under the new 100-1 law, a law Congress passed without any hearings, crack dealers were singled out for harsh punishment. A dealer selling $50,000 worth of powder would do the same time as a dealer selling $750 worth of crack. This was a law specifically designed to attack and blame the poorest and most vulnerable for government policy. This is not a new tactic. Check out my first two books; the US government has been attacking its own citizens using these methods for a century plus.

In contrast to the government and media's position on crack, drug expert Steven Belenko at the time said,

"One interesting aspect of the anti-crack crusade is that it occurred in the presence of a real vacuum of knowledge about the drug." He also said, "During the period of strongest concern over crack, 1986-1990, crack was actually the least-used drug among all illicit drugs."

Really? How can the AP, NYT, and other respectable pillars of journalistic truth print blatant lies like "crack is becoming the nation's drug of choice" when it can be disproven at the time when they wrote it? These outlets are not journalists; they are propagandists.

"Researchers were finding crack to be not a national problem, but a phenomenon isolated to the inner cities or less than a dozen urban areas," drug expert James Inciardi said in 1987.

Eventually, even the DEA admitted the hype was not real. Strange, we didn't see this in mainstream media at the time? According to the DEA in 1986, "Crack is currently the subject of considerable media attention. The result has been a distortion of the public perception of the extent of crack use as compared to the use of other drugs. Crack presently appears to be a secondary rather than a primary problem in most areas."

And don't kid yourselves. The media and the government work hand-in-hand when it comes to creating and distributing this bigoted propaganda intended to support the ruling classes' repression of the lower classes. If you think publications like the New York Times are the shining light of democracy and journalism, think again; they partnered tightly with the federal government in parroting the company line on drugs like crack.

It was Robert Stutman, the Chief of the NY DEA office, who created the PR crack campaign to amplify the issue and secure funding. The PR campaign worked so well that it sparked a frenzy of media coverage of crack across all major outlets. Mainstream media shifted the public stance on illegal drugs considerably, which is what they are there to do. Before the crack PR campaign, only 2% of Americans thought drugs were America's top problem. After the PR campaign and media frenzy, 13% thought drugs were our #1 problem. Look how effective **propaganda** is. No wonder this is how the government and the owner class shift public opinion, not with truth and values, but with state-sponsored and media-coordinated propaganda campaigns.

At the time, drug researchers Golub and Hartman found that the majority of drug information appearing in the *New York Times*, *Newsweek*, and *Time* came only from two sources – cops and politicians (aka the people who had the most to gain from a drug panic). Actual drug researchers and academics were rarely quoted or cited in major media outlets. *The New York Times* is one of the biggest offenders. Fewer than one in ten *New York Times* stories about crack had an expert opinion. This handpicked selection of biased commentary is a key tactic in manufacturing consent on a variety of issues across the population.

It is interesting to note that the crack hysteria continued through the elections at the time until a bigger story broke. That story was quite embarrassing to US leadership and brings us right back to the Contras.

"It was not until the revelations about Lieutenant Colonel Oliver L. North and the Iran-Contra connection toward the close of 1986 that crack media coverage experienced significant declines," said drug researcher Inciardi.

BY the spring of 1986, the Contras (remember them?) were almost out of money. While Oliver North and his crew were able to replace some of the CIA's lost funding with donations from Saudi Arabia and Taiwan (that was nice of them), it just wasn't enough. It turns out it's expensive to feed, train, arm, and equip a whole army. The Contras' food bill ranged from $1 million to $2 million per month. It's estimated that the Contra war cost between $100 million and $200 million annually.

In response to escalating costs, the White House tried to get Congress to turn the money back on for the Contras, for about $100 million per year. When the Congressional committee looked into it, they found lots of evidence that Contra leaders were corrupt, dealing drugs and weapons, using US supply lines to run both, and that some US government officials were protecting them.

"We can produce specific law enforcement officials who will tell you that they have been called off drug trafficking investigations because the CIA is involved or because it would threaten national security or because the State Department did not want it to happen," Senator John Kerry told the committee. "Our sources have suggested in direct testimony that agencies of the United States government may be failing to stop or punish those engaging in these criminal activities because those individuals are otherwise engaged in helping United States foreign policy."

Kerry's chief investigator said that "the narcotics are coming into the United States not by the pound, not by the bag, but by the ton, by the cargo planeload."

Senator John Kerry provided a list of areas that Congress needed to investigate further. They included the murder of Dr. Hugo Spottiforo by the Contras.

"An ongoing drug smuggling operation connecting Columbia, Costa Rica, Nicaragua, and the United States, in which the Contra and American supporters, with the apparent knowledge of the Contra leadership, handled the transport of cocaine produced in Columbia, shipped to Costa Rica, processed in the region, transported to airstrips controlled by American supporters of the Contras," and "Allegations that have surfaced regarding other drug smuggling operations involving shrimp boats operating out of Texas, Louisiana, and Florida."
– Senator John Kerry

Wow. All that right from the mouth of a sitting US Senator. How's that for confirmation?

Things started leaking to the press, and publications like the *San Francisco Examiner* ran stories about some of the Contra/CIA drug deals that went south. These stories were attacked by the state as expected, with blatant lies, denouncing the idea that the Contras were smuggling drugs and that the government was looking the other way. Soon, another story in the *Examiner* exposed Norwin Meneses's cocaine trafficking network and his involvement with the Contras and the CIA. But even though these stories came out right before the hearings on the Contra aid packages, not a single major media outlet picked them up. Strange huh? I mean, if these companies were really the trusted shining lights of democracy as they have claimed, surely, they would be interested in this story?

This reminds me of when legendary US journalist Seymore Hersh exposed the US for committing the most egregious terrorist attack in history when it blew up its ally's Nordstream pipeline during the Ukrainian War. That story, as of this writing, has not appeared in one major new publication. In fact,

The New York Times, with zero supporting evidence, claimed a Ukrainian splinter group committed the act. Another notable story like this was the Hunter Biden laptop videos, where Hunter was caught smoking crack with hookers in a hotel room, which was buried by every major news network and suppressed to assist in Biden's appointment to the Presidency. How is that working out for everyone?

Now things started to break really badly. At the time, a customs informant was trying to sell illegal weapons to Iraq and was caught in a sting by US Customs agents. During the interview, this informant claimed he had "hard-core, documentable, bring-it-into-court information" on DEA criminal drug activity.

Six witnesses, all US and Costa Rica officials, were willing to testify that DEA agents were skimming cocaine from drug seizures, making counterfeit money, sanitizing intelligence reports to Washington, and protecting cocaine processing labs in northern Costa Rica at two Contra bases.

At the end of July 1986, the informant had enough information about the DEA's criminal activities and hand-delivered it on a microcassette. He told Customs, "That the DEA agents in Costa Rica knew the location of drug laboratories and had been paid to conceal the location of the narcotics." After this, the informant claimed the DEA was trying to assassinate him. The informant said, "I think the DEA people are trying to kill me. I am convinced that they were involved in narcotics trafficking and looking the other way."

Now, more law officers were starting to investigate the Contra drug and gun operation. Still, strangely enough, those investigations, although they led to the convictions of kingpins like Danilo Blandon, were never pursued. An LA police officer who filed an affidavit on the Contra drug/gun operation stated, "The investigation centers around a male Nicaraguan named Danilo Blandon. The Blandon organization is believed to be moving hundreds of kilos of cocaine a month in the Southern California area, and the money is laundered through a variety of business fronts and then sent to Florida, where the money goes toward the purchase of arms to aid the Contra rebels fighting the civil war in Nicaragua." He also mentioned that a corrupt ex-cop named Ronald Lister, known to be an illegal heavy-weapon dealer, was involved.

Lister wasn't happy about being questioned and told investigators, "You don't know what you're doing. There's a bigger picture here. I'm working for the CIA. I know the director of the CIA in Los Angeles. The government is allowing drug sales to go on in the United States."

When Danilo Blandon was investigated, documents concerning him turned up at his house, according to the Justice Department Inspector General. "Some of these deposits were marked 'U.S. Treasury/State and totaled approximately $9,000,000. Other deposits were marked Cayman Islands and totaled about $883,000." Not a problem, though, for the Contras and the CIA. Mr. Blandon was set free after the investigation; he was tipped off by informants first, so nothing of consequence was found.

After the raids, within a few days, the investigating officers were told that CIA agents had come into their offices and taken all the records the cops had seized during the arrest. Not only did the documents disappear, but so did the evidence and the original police reports.

Even when famous drug smuggler Barry Seal's old plane was shot down over Nicaragua, carrying a load of weapons, which in fact was part of Oliver North's resupply operation, the White House, CIA, and State Department all denied the cargo plane had any connection to the US government. The tactic of admitting nothing and denying everything is the bread and butter of authoritarian regimes everywhere.

Even more interesting, according to the LA Sheriff's Office, within days of the raid, all the evidence was given back to Blandon and Lister. I'm sure they received an apology, too. Any remaining evidence was destroyed within six months of the investigation's closure. Federal agents placed the Sheriff's office's original affidavit under court seal to prevent it from becoming public. Eventually, the affidavit disappeared from the Sheriff's office, too. Soon, Blandon walked free and was told the case had been dropped and that no charges would be filed.

None of this mattered at all, apparently, to the Reagan administration or the US Congress, as after a 2-year break in funding, Reagan signed a bill authorizing the CIA to spend $100 million a year on the Contras. Woohoo!

But wait, it's not time to celebrate yet. At this time, President Ronald Reagan and Attorney General Edwin Meese announced to the media that millions of dollars from the sale of missiles to the Iranian government (our sworn enemy, then and now, who had kidnapped American embassy workers) had been illegally diverted to the Contras by Lt. Col. Oliver North. This began the official Iran-Contra investigation and scandal with the code word "Operation Front Door".

The FBI investigated and found no connection between Lister and the Iran-Contra scandal. Huh. But when American reporters went down to Central America looking for a story, they found plenty of evidence linking Oliver North, the White House, and the CIA to illegal Contra supply activities.

In 1986, Costa Rica's biggest newspaper published a series on the Contras' connections to drug trafficking, focusing on Norwin Meneses, the DEA's top informant and the CIA's top cocaine importer to South LA drug gangs.

Once it was fully exposed, all the US operations in Costa Rica were abandoned, and the Costa Rican government began arresting Contras for violating their neutrality.

WITH all this evidence and information coming out, with huge national news stories and investigations into the Iran-Contra scandal, only one thing could be done, and that would not involve any actual investigations or justice.

Quickly, the Justice Department dropped the criminal investigation into Contra cocaine sales in LA, and the whole case was made **TOP SECRET** and buried for the next ten years. This was until investigative journalist Gary Webb found all this information, only to lose his life and career for bringing it to you.

But that did not stop the LA police from going after all those black crack dealers in LA. We pretend that they are not getting their drugs from the CIA and their goons, and blame them for the crimes of our government and leadership. Nice fall guys. Here is what one LA detective has to say about Ricky Ross, LA's biggest crack dealer.

"What he did, he poisoned tens of thousands of people. He overdosed them. He killed them. There are a lot of crack babies out there now because of him."

Interesting. I guess the same could be said of the DEA, the CIA, the State Department, the Reagan administration, the LAPD, and Meneses and Blandon. But let's blame the black guys from the hood. It's all their fault for trying to survive their horrible, impoverished existences.

Just to give you an idea of what tactics the LAPD deployed when harassing and arresting black drug dealers, they were accused of beatings, theft, property destruction, and false arrests. Nice guys, huh? Who exactly are the criminals here? Let the white-collar criminals walk free, and pat them on the back, while throwing the book at lower-end black dealers—our heroes.

None of this stopped the Nicaraguan cocaine smuggling operation. All the police and intelligence agencies from the LAPD, the LA Sheriff's Department, the FBI, the CIA, the DEA, and the IRS were fully aware of the Contra-cocaine operation. But nothing stopped it. They just moved some leaders around and kept right on going.

And with all the competition for cocaine dealing in the LA area, prices were dropping, and profits were thinning. Hence, dealers needed opportunities and moved to other places to continue moving product.

"Los Angeles drug gangs are spreading cocaine and violence in cities nationwide and may become a new form of organized crime unless they are stopped soon," an AP story said in 1988. "Authorities say, members of two prominent rival drug gangs from LA, the Crips and the Bloods, have infiltrated cities from Alaska to Washington, DC." Thanks to the CIA, DEA, and other supposed 'good guys' for that one. These black drug gangs not only got their coke from the CIA-protected smugglers, but they also bought their guns, listening devices, and other high-end hardware from CIA contractors. The 1988 drug craze backlash was 100% targeted at the drug gangs like the Crips and the Bloods, and no mention in any media outlets of where and who they got their drugs and assault rifles from.

How bad were the cops in LA then?

"This may be a terrible thing to say, but as we got into this thing, it became obvious that the stories being told by the crooks were more credible than the stories being told by our officers," said the LA County Sheriff.

In the end, it became clear that the cops were not policing anything; they were using new asset seizure laws to rip off drug dealers and take their possessions and money. In 1988, the Sheriff's office took in $33.9 million in cash, 66 houses, 110 vehicles, four airplanes, and two businesses. It seems the narcotics detectives were just criminals themselves.

As the feds were looking into police misconduct in LA, a police officer informant told the feds that the LA narcotics task force had routinely beaten suspects, planted drugs, lied in court, falsified search warrant affidavits, and stolen drug money by skimming off the top of seized cash.

These cops went out and bought vacation homes, big-screen TVs, jewelry, new cars, boats, helicopters, plastic surgery, parties, and vacations. In 1990, a federal grand jury indicted ten deputies on 27 counts of theft, income tax evasion, and conspiracy. It was in a trial for one of these corrupt cops that his defense attorney linked stolen cash to the Contras and the CIA. Uh oh.

In this totally supposedly unrelated trial, documents and details of the cop's raid on Ronald Lister, the ex-cop arms dealer, came to light. They included "Films of military operations in Central America, technical manuals, information on assorted military hardware and communications, and numerous documents indicating drug money was being used to purchase military equipment for Central America. Officers also pieced together the fact that this suspect was also working with the Blandon family, which was importing narcotics from Central America into the United States."

See the trouble leadership faces with things like this coming out in court, which creates a public record and makes it hard to hide. No worries, the prosecution filed a motion to "exclude any questions, testimony, or other evidence relating to any alleged CIA plot to launder drug money to finance Nicaraguan operations or operations in Iran." The judge agreed and threatened to gag the defense attorney if he complained. Jurors were told to disregard any of this testimony.

Part of what was going on was that the CIA was attacking the police for going after their drug guy, Danilo Blandon. According to one detective, "Every policeman who ever got close to Blandon was either told to back off, investigated by their department, forced to retire, or indicted." Don't be too concerned; in the end, the cops all walked free for police abuse and corruption. It should be no surprise to people nowadays.

Even though combat between the Contras and Sandinistas ceased in March 1988 with a truce, the CIA continued its covert war to destabilize the Sandinista government, leveraging their assets like Meneses and Blandon to do so. Blandon would be repeatedly not prosecuted for his crimes while he turned informant and collaborator with the DEA. Even when the largest drug bust in Nicaraguan history was made and linked to Meneses, the US support of him never wavered. It turns out Meneses, just like Danilo, was a DEA snitch and informant, and was working with the CIA to try to set up Sandinista officials in a drug sting. Meneses was arrested in Nicaragua for drug smuggling, with zero help from the US intelligence or DEA, and was released only 7 years later.

There would be no comeuppance for these criminals.

THE incredibly well-researched and detailed information you read in part three is from journalist Gary Webb, who wrote the book used as source material. Gary was one of the most dedicated and professional journalists in the US media in the last 50 years. For his tireless dedication to finding the truth and holding power accountable, he had his life and career destroyed not just by the people he was trying to expose, but also by their propaganda outlets, *The New York Times*, *The Washington Post*, and the *LA Times*.

In 1998, the CIA was onto Gary's investigation, and released the following cables from the CIA Inspector General's report called "Possible Attempts to Link CIA to Narcotraffickers." It said, "In November 1995, we were informed by the DEA that a reporter had been inquiring about activities in Central America and any links with the Contras. DEA has been alerted that Meneses will undoubtedly claim that he was trafficking narcotics on behalf of the CIA to generate money for the Contras."

According to Gary Webb, "The series will show that the dumping of cocaine on LA's street gangs was the back end of a covert effort to arm and equip the CIA's ragtag army of anti-Communist Contra guerrillas. While there has long been solid – if largely ignored – evidence of a CIA-Contra-cocaine connection, no one has ever asked the question: "Where did all the cocaine go once it got here? Now we know."

Gary was 100% right. It's all in documented transcripts; they cannot deny. The Contras sold drugs on an industrial scale to American citizens, mainly black Americans, and the CIA had protected them, supplied them, and given them direction to do so.

The War on Drugs is the height of American hypocrisy. The street crack dealers were held accountable and sent to prison, while the men who imported and sold them the cocaine walked away scot-free, with government protection, just like the mafia does. It was the CIA/Contras who, in the early 1980s, began the crack epidemic by supplying the ghettos with unlimited cheap cocaine, ending in the 1990s with anti-crack laws sending thousands of blacks to prison.

"The fact that a government-connected drug ring was dumping tons of cocaine into the black neighborhoods in LA – and to a lesser extent, San Jose, Oakland, San Francisco, Portland, Houston, Oklahoma City, Alabama, and New Orleans – goes a long way towards explaining why crack developed such deep roots in the black community," said Gary Webb.

Gary knew that this would be a groundbreaking story that would get a lot of pushback and denial from the government, CIA, and, of course, corporate-controlled media, like the *Washington Post* and *Time*. For example, in 1974, the New York Times reported that Seymour Hersh, the investigative journalist who exposed the USA's terrorist bombing of the Nordstream pipeline, wrote an expose on Operation CHAOS, a massive illegal CIA domestic spying operation against American citizens. His story was attacked, just as Gary's was by the same propagandists, as the *Washington Post* said, "he has no hard proof." Time said, "There is a strong likelihood that Hersh's CIA story is considerably exaggerated." A CBS newsman who leaked a Congressional report on CIA abuses was fired and blackballed from journalism, just like what happened to any journalist who investigated the Contra drug smuggling operation.

Soon after the Mercury News story was published on the CIA/Contra cocaine/guns smuggling operation, establishment media outlets lined up to parrot the CIA version of the story and undermine and bash the legitimate reporting of Webb's story. Just like they did today regarding Hersh's Nordstream story, all of the media outlets agreed that the facts of Webb's story were accurate, but his conclusions were wrong. Were they? You just heard all the evidence. Seems pretty open-and-shut to me.

Maybe the reason has to do with the fact that many establishment reporters are actually CIA stooges on the dole. For example, Walter Pincus, a veteran national security reporter for the *Washington Post,* wrote a story slamming Webb's investigative journalism, arguing that the data does not support the claims.

Well, it turns out Walter Pincus wrote a story in 1967 titled "How I Traveled Abroad on CIA Subsidy." In it, Pincus said he posed as a student representative and infiltrated international youth conferences in the late 50s and early 60s, gathering info for the CIA and smuggling in anti-Communist propaganda. He said a CIA recruiter had approached him, and he agreed to spy on both foreign and American students. Nice guy, huh? This supposed leading journalist is actually an admitted CIA operative and propagandist. And this was the 1960s folks, imagine how sophisticated and ingrained they are in media now?

On the MacNeil/Lehrer NewsHour in 1986, Pincus said of repressing government information, "We've been dealing with it for a long time, and I think we have withheld a great deal of information. It ought to be made clear to people that we, in determining what we're going to do with a lot of stories, go to the administration and tell them what we have and listen to what their arguments are, and we then make a decision, but we're not making them in the dark."

How interesting that the stories in response to Webb's articles all seemed to have the same rationale and shared talking points. The LA Times said, "The crack epidemic in LA followed no blueprint or master plan. It was not orchestrated by the Contras or the CIA."

According to Gary Webb,

"The government side of the story is coming through the Los Angeles Times, The New York Times, and The Washington Post. They use the giant corporate press rather than saying anything directly. If you work through friendly reporters on major newspapers, it comes off as The New York Times saying it and not a mouthpiece of the CIA."

Sadly, this experience taught Gary that the US independent press isn't quite as free and independent as he thought.

"If we had met five years ago, you wouldn't have found a stauncher defender of the newspaper industry than me ... And then I wrote some stories that made me realize how sadly misplaced my bliss had been," he said. "The reason I'd enjoyed such smooth sailing for so long hadn't been, as I'd assumed, because I was careful and diligent and good at my job ... The truth was that, in all those years, I hadn't written anything important enough to suppress."

Wow, now that is some hardcore honesty. Too bad some Americans can't be so honest with themselves.

Furthermore, in an essay, Gary states that he believed there was an active "collusion between the press and the powerful" to report freely on inconsequential matters, "but when it comes to the real down and dirty stuff…We begin to see the limits of our freedoms."

This wasn't just Gary's opinion. Bob Parry, the AP reporter who first broke the Contra story in 1985 and then backed away, sent him this note. "Like you, I grew up in this business thinking our job really was to tell the public the truth. Maybe that was the mission at one time. But something has happened to the media in the 1980s. Part of it was the pressure from public diplomacy on the outside. But part of it was the smug, snotty, sophomoric crowd that came to dominate the national media from the inside. These characters fell in love with their power to define reality, not their responsibility to uncover hard facts. By the 1990s, the media had become the monster."

For all his hard work, dedication, and efforts to show truth to the American people, on December 10, 2004, Gary Webb mysteriously and supposedly committed suicide by shooting himself twice in the head. Did you hear that? The coroner and establishment claim he somehow shot himself in the head twice, not once. That would be quite a trick for someone to pull off.

Did the CIA assassinate Gary for his Dark Alliance series? I guess if you believe Jeffrey Epstein killed himself, you may think the same here.

The reality is that Gary's work and research were second to none. According to California Representative Maxine Waters, "Gary's documentation is awesome, and his work ethic is unbelievable." She stated that, upon Webb's death, he was "one of the finest investigative journalists that our country has ever seen."

There would be no comeuppance for the CIA, or anyone involved in these broad and audacious crimes. A CIA internal probe found the agency was not at fault. In fact, it was determined during hearings that there was a secret agreement between the CIA and the Justice Department to look the other way on drug dealing with non-CIA employees (aka the Contras). It was a nice *don't ask, don't tell policy* that let drug runners act with legal impunity.

It was all based on Ronald Reagan's Executive Order No. 12333. According to journalist Robert Parry, this executive order was signed just as the CIA was getting involved in the Contra project and conflict in Afghanistan, and this legal loophole protected narcotics traffickers working on behalf of intelligence agencies. "They could only have been done for one purpose. They were anticipating what would eventually happen. They knew drugs were going to be sold."

As a final side note to this sad and tragic story, in December 1998, Manuel Noriega, (remember him? Evil dictator drug trafficker that we had to invade Panama so we could bring him to justice) appealed for a reduction to his 40-year prison sentence for drug trafficking and money laundering, Lucky for him, he had an enthusiastic supporter to vouch for him; Donald Winters, former chief of CIA operations in Panama. He told the judge that Noriega had performed valuable work for the US and we should give him a break.

The ex-CIA chief said –

"Noriega brokered deals with South American leaders, acted as a liaison to Cuba's Fidel Castro, provided details on guerrilla and terrorist activities, and even gave the former Shah of Iran a safe haven. There were specific instances when the US government worked through General Noriega."

Wow, isn't that nice to get such kind words and support from the CIA and the US government? Of course, in March 1999, his jail sentence was reduced from 40 years to 10 years, making him eligible for parole within a year. Woo-hoo! Interesting how this monster, whom we had to invade Panama to stop his crimes, could be set free almost immediately with the blessing and OK from the US government. Were black LA drug dealers given the same latitude? I think you know the answer to that question.

WHAT is the drug war? First, let's talk about what the drug war is not.

It is not a public health policy. If it were, it would be applied equally and fairly across all segments of society. It would also be equally and fairly applied across all drugs, not just the ones certain ultra-rich people don't like. Finally, it would be backed up by real-world substantiated data that said the drug war was, in fact, good for people's health and society overall.

Second, the drug war is not a moral or religious crusade against the evils of drug use and addiction, for if it were, it would also be equally applied across all strata of society. The laws and enforcement framework would be trying to target all people guilty of implied drug vices, not just the poor, brown, and left-leaning ones. The targeted and selective application of legal enforcement and punishment exposes the true nature and goals of the drug war.

The drug war is a tool and tactic to leverage power and control over specific individuals and groups deemed undesirable by the owner and ruling classes. You can more specifically call the drug war an expression and extension of the white supremacy power structure, which has been managing the world since the **Invasion of the New World** over 500 years ago. This expression and implementation of white supremacy over Asian, African, and native peoples began in the colonial era and continues to this day.

In part one of *The Drug to Control,* we began by explaining how it was the Western colonial powers that addicted the world's population to what are now called illicit drugs. They used violence and their military to open up China and Southeast Asia to opium shipping and distribution, conquering Asia and dividing it up into spheres and colonies for exploitation. In this, they subjected and drove millions of native peoples to drug addiction, creating an endless source of revenue and profit for the European owner and ruling class.

The genesis of the drug war began in the 1500s when European merchants introduced opium smoking to natives in their captive colonies. In the 1700s, the British East India Company became the first large-scale opium smuggler, forcibly supplying opium to an unwilling China that did not want its people turned into junked-out zombies. By the 1800s, the supply chain was complete, and every European colony worldwide had state-run opium dens that accounted for a significant share of revenue from those colonies.

Before the first Portuguese ships, which brought opiates to the native populations, opium smoking and the opium trade were not well-developed in Asia. It was Europe's Age of Discovery, a nice euphemism for **Europe's Age of Subjugation and Conquest**, that not coincidentally coincided with the start of Asia's modern opium trade. The two events are closely related and integral to each other.

The objective is to conquer people who lack the military or technology to resist, then take over their land and economies to extract wealth and resources from them and ship them back to the colonial powers, impoverishing those people and making them unwilling subjects of their respective empires. Then, since you have already stolen their resources and enslaved their people, you addict their population to opium so you can extract more wealth and subservience out of these poor people you abused and used, further enslaving them to your will.

This is the superior culture that brought enlightenment and modernization to the developing world? Please.

The global opium market and trade were a direct result of European colonialism, and would not have existed or developed as they did without it.

In the mid-19th century, the ruling elite of the European powers decided there was tremendous wealth to be extracted from poor third-world nations to their more advanced economies, so they started annexing these countries and integrating them, by force, into their global empires. These countries and their native people could now be controlled through economic oppression, not just force. This financial and social repression was enacted when the colonialists allied themselves with the native elites to suppress social forces and labor movements, such as unions and leftist intellectuals.

For instance, when the US replaced the French in Indochina in 1955, we spent the next 20 years shoring up corrupt oligarchies and keeping reformers out of power. If you doubt this process, take a look at Central America and the Caribbean, and see how all those people have been kept for decades by their colonial oppressor, the USA.

It was the US-based pharmaceutical companies like Bayer and Merck that created modern synthetic drugs like heroin and cocaine, and their mass advertising of these drugs to the general public is what addicted the world's population to their poisonous concoctions. They advertised these drugs as non-addictive and lied to millions of people to make them think addictive drugs were OK to take and give to their kids. Doctors were only too happy to parrot this lie, and they were used to convince people that these drugs were safe.

The mass marketing of cocaine and heroin is what created mass addiction across the global population.

These drugs were pushed onto the general populace not just for profit for big pharma, but to keep them jacked up and working during their wage-slave 12-hour/7-day work schedules in the USA's factories.

By the early 20th century, the enlightened Western powers were starting to look really bad in their exploitation and abuse of their colonies and native peoples. Even worse, all those harmful drugs they pushed on poor natives were coming back home, and more upper-class white people were getting high on opium and other compounds. This was too much for the white supremacist Christian crusaders to tolerate. They were just fine with exploiting and abusing savages with drugs, but friendly white people, not so much.

This led to the 20th-century drug war, which, as described in detail in this book, morphed into a vehicle far removed from its original intent. It developed almost immediately as a method to generate revenue for off-the-books military adventures (black ops) so countries like the USA and France could continue to do horrible things in our own and other countries without any trace or accountability.

To protect those covert military operations, for decades, the CIA operated above the law and above any accountability to act as a Mafioso enforcer for international drug dealers working in concert with US political objectives. US drug agencies like the DEA were only pointed in the direction that was the most politically and economically beneficial to US interests, at countries and governments not playing ball with the US on the world stage.

The drug war immediately became intertwined with the fanatical anti-Communism crusade in the US. Shameless opportunists like FBN Director Harry J. Anslinger and CIA Director Allen Dulles tried to link international drug smuggling, usually falsely, to Communists, when in fact, it was the pro-business Capitalists and their cronies in the mafia who were primarily leveraging and benefiting from the drug war. This rationale was used time and time again for illegal operations and criminal activities against supposedly left-leaning or Communist/Socialist-led nations.

The CIA and the US government have had a close working relationship and partnership with the Italian and Corsican mafia since WW2. The mafia was instrumental in working with the Allies in the invasion of Italy, and the US helped set up Italian mobsters as respectable leaders in post-fascist Italy. Once mobsters like Lucky Luciano were deported from the US, they were allowed to set up global drug smuggling operations from Italy and France with the protection and support of the CIA. The US worked closely with the mob on a variety of illegal operations, from drug manufacturing, distribution, and smuggling, to the assassination of world leaders like JFK, Patrice Lumumba of the Congo, and attempts on Fidel Castro.

It really was the fall of the nationalist Chinese government to a Communist revolution that set the Golden Triangle in motion as the world's major opium/heroin supplier. The US/Truman administration sent in support and arms to the exiled government hiding out in Burma. The US government established the Golden Triangle trade zone to fund its clandestine operations and military activities.

Opium warlords in Southeast Asia used CIA resources, including arms, ammunition, and mainly air transport to move an industrial scale number of drugs, allowing them to increase their power and control over their respective communities. The CIA fully embraced and supported regional drug lords and actively enabled them to increase their power with its support. In the end, as the drug warlords' power from opium profits increased, so did the CIA's combat and power capacities.

By 1973, twenty years after the CIA first began supporting national KMT troops after the Chinese Communist Revolution, in the *Golden Triangle,* the KMT produced 1/3 of the entire world's opium supply, thanks to the support, airpower, and funding of the CIA and US government.

In part two of *The Drug to Control,* we moved on from how drugs were used to fund clandestine operations and off-the-books anti-Communist activities to how they were used within intelligence agencies like the CIA to engage in programs of mind control over individuals and groups, including unwitting US citizens. How do we know the CIA was targeting US citizens with mind control? From the CIA itself. In a memo dated July 13, 1951, the CIA describes its mind-control efforts as,

"Broad and comprehensive, involving both **domestic** and overseas activities."

From its inception, the CIA was empowered with such broad authority that it operated above the law and independent of the executive branch and congressional oversight. From the first day the CIA was in existence, they began operations on US soil that were criminal and in direct conflict with their charter and US law to develop mind control programs.

It is critical to know that the USA, in part, got the idea for its psychedelic drug mind control program from Nazi scientists who performed their unethical experiments on unwilling concentration camp prisoners at Dachau, Germany. The very scientists and doctors who ran this program for the Nazis were brought to the USA after the war in **Operation Paperclip** to serve in the highest roles of NASA and other agencies. Nazi doctors and scientists and their research formed the basis of the USA's mind control program, eventually designated MK-ULTRA.

In this, the horrific experiments in Nazi Germany that were put on trial at Nuremberg were brought over lock, stock, and barrel to the US post-WW2, where US citizens now served as the unwilling guinea pigs in these Nazi doctors' sick experiments. US doctors and medical leaders were only too happy to pick up this work in the name of anti-Communism and follow in the steps of their Nazi forbearers, usually working side by side with ex-Nazi scientists. This work went on for decades and involved the highest levels of the medical and psychiatric establishment.

And just like the Nazi doctors whom they followed in their experiments, the CIA victimized vulnerable groups as unwilling test subjects in their experiments, including prisoners, the mentally ill, the terminally ill, LGBTQ, and ethnic minorities. These are primarily the poor people the drug war is targeted at, time and time again. In the greatest of irony and hypocrisy, the very doctors who sat as judges on the Nuremberg trials, condemning Nazi doctors, were themselves performing the very same experiments on unwitting US citizens.

It was during the reign of Allen Dulles over the CIA that drug mind control programs were formalized and expanded, and would continue for at least the next few decades until they were forced to move more underground and overseas after congressional hearings in the 1970s. Before the hearings began, Dulles and his cronies made sure to destroy almost all evidence around MK-ULTRA, so what has remained is heavily redacted and just a taste of much more significant crimes against humanity.

Experiments in drug-induced mind control were just the beginning for the US intelligence and military community. They were interested in LSD for psycho-chemical warfare (cool band name, right?) to dose entire cities before an invasion. There was also a contingency plan to use BZ (an LSD horror drug) on the US population in case of civilian insurrection. Are you looking forward to that, everyone?

The great irony of the CIA's mind control program is that it was so widespread in distributing LSD and other psychedelics in research settings and tests that it became popular with famous LSD users and advocates like Ken Kesey and Timothy Leary. This led to an explosion in LSD usage among youth, intellectuals, artists, and activist groups, altering the fabric of American society in the late 60s. It can be argued that the widespread use of LSD led to significantly more unrest and subversion in the US, all thanks to the CIA. Fascinating. The very people who are tasked with protecting US society are, in fact, the ones undermining it.

The media partnered with the CIA every step of the way on LSD. First, they promoted it when the CIA was all HIGH on it, thinking it was the solution to all their sick dreams. This initial promotion of LSD/psychedelics by Time/Life is what interested Dr. Timothy Leary in it and began his journey. Ken Kesey was a subject in the CIA LSD MK-ULTRA experiments, and he snuck some out to turn on his friends to help kick-start the 1960s psychedelic revolution.

In 1962, LSD began to fall out of favor with the establishment as the CIA shifted its behavioral research activities towards operations and away from long-range studies. Then, once the CIA moved onto BZ as its primary incapacitating chemical agent, LSD was vilified, first in the CIA-friendly media sphere by intelligence assets like Time-Life, then through legislation and law.

In just the course of 5 years, LSD went from a miracle drug for the new millennium to the worst thing ever, calling LSD "the greatest threat facing the country today…more dangerous than the Vietnam War." Sadly, there would be no data or evidence to support these statements. In fact, the data showed the opposite. Luckily, that information was never released to the public through our moral-crusading media establishment.

The illegalization of LSD follows a pretty standard playbook for power and control. The government and private enterprises push drugs on people for a variety of objectives (profit, control, etc.), then, when those drugs become embarrassing as they penetrate the upper strata of society, those drugs are vilified and illegalized. Lower-class people are held accountable for the crimes of their leaders.

All of this control and oversight really only applied to certain drugs used by certain people, which exposes the true purpose and objective of the drug war – Individual and group control. In the late 60s, the groups that needed to be controlled better were white middle and upper-class students and youth, and black militants. So, illegalizing LSD and psychedelics and upping the stakes in the overall drug war allowed the government and ruling class to target these dissidents without looking like the authoritarian oppressors they really are.

To accomplish this level of repression and control, FBI agents were trained to infiltrate hippies. FBI agent provocateurs, dressed as hippies or student radicals, would start riots or burn flags to incite more violence and provoke negative media attention and public reaction. They continue to do the same things during other large-scale protests, like the Black Lives Matter protests. But it wasn't just the FBI spying and persecuting American youth; it was the IRS, DEA, FCC, local and state police, and frankly, the whole government has been turned against the US public from the 1970s onward.

These secret police activities were formalized and expanded into Operation CHAOS when Nixon authorized them. As part of this operation, in addition to monitoring left-wing organizations, the CIA provided training, technical assistance, equipment, and intelligence to local police departments on political dissidents.

Yes, it is a fact. The FBI is, in part, a secret police force targeted at left-of-center activists and workers' rights advocates. Their other work dealing with serial killers and bank robbers is just a cover for their real goals and objectives—the repression and suppression of dissidence in the United States of America.

The use of drugs to incapacitate or modify the behavior of American citizens is proven by the CIA's own memos. Just because the last time we were allowed to hear about it was in the 70s doesn't mean it stopped; it just moved more clandestinely and underground.

The CIA and colluding elements of the medical, psychiatric, and military institutions first introduced and pushed LSD and other drugs on the American people, without their knowledge and consent. Then, once their objectives were accomplished, they attacked and vilified the very people they turned onto those same drugs. This vilification had nothing to do with public health, individual well-being, or some social-moral imperative, and everything to do with the repression, suppression, and criminalization of dissidents and politically undesirable citizens.

In part three, *The Drug to Control* moved onto the 1980s, when the framework and supply chain that created the Golden Triangle global heroin industry, which in turn helped to hook millions of US citizens and servicemen on junk, was relocated to central and southern America, with cocaine replacing heroin and opium as the drug of choice to topple legitimate governments and frame popular leftist groups like the Sandinistas.

After the US-aligned government of Nicaragua collapsed, led for decades by the horrible dictator Somoza, the CIA and

Reagan administration created the Contras, a paramilitary terrorist, drug, and arms smuggling organization, from the ground up, which was staffed by ex-Somoza terrorists, criminals, and goons. You know, the type of people who assassinate archbishops during Sunday mass.

At first, the CIA and the Reagan administration had lots of money to fund the Contras. From 1981 to 1984, the CIA ran the Contra operation directly, giving out weapons and money, hiring subcontractors, transporting supplies, and doing strategy and tactics. But the CIA and Contras got a little too aggressive with mining their harbors and started blowing up US-allies' shipping. After this incident, all CIA funding for the Contras was cut off by Congress.

Following this, the CIA/Contras turned to smuggling and dealing cocaine at scale to fund and arm their burgeoning terrorist army, just like they had done in Southeast Asia with Vietnamese Hmong tribesmen during the 1950s-1970s. Once we pulled out of our so-called anti-Communist (more like taxpayer money laundering) activities in Vietnam, the drug lords in Southeast Asia were arrested. At the same time, we set up new drug lords in Central America to rerun the whole process. Eventually, just like the Vietnamese opium/heroin lords we propped up and then tore down, we would do the same to loyal CIA partners like international drug kingpin General Manuel Noriega.

Working with the CIA to bring in planeloads of cocaine into the USA and into LA were top-level drug dealers Danilo Blando and Norwin Meneses. Also working with them are everyone from ex-LA police officers to hard-up Indian tribes.

The massive influx of affordable cocaine helped to create local kingpins in the crack market, like Ricky Ross. Ricky and other black people from the ghetto would be the villains in this manufactured drama. While Ricky got his drugs directly from

Blandon and Meneses, he would be the only one to see his life ruined and destroyed by his business activities. The white people who sold him drugs, guns, and equipment would all walk scot-free.

To get funding for the Contras and ensure future support, the CIA worked with its allies in the media to distribute propaganda stories and run psyops campaigns against the American public.

The CIA and the National Security Council engaged in "a domestic, covert operation designed to lobby the Congress, manipulate the media and influence domestic public opinion," the report said, supporting another 1987 investigation which said the State Department had engaged in "prohibited, covert propaganda activities."

Do you think it's possible these types of propaganda and psyops never stopped, but continued and have been refined and optimized over the past 30-40 years? Why would they have stopped? There was nothing but some top-secret congressional oversight meetings, not actual action that couldn't be easily subverted. Not until Gary Webb wrote his book was any of this information made public, and Gary quickly lost his life for doing his job. Real journalism is a death sentence in a certain type of society we appear to live in.

Remember that international drug dealing is primarily being supported by US intelligence as a method for generating revenue for illegal military operations, which is what the Contras became once funding was cut by Congress. And to fund entire armies in the field, you must deal lots and lots of cocaine. Planeloads of cocaine. Enough cocaine to supply the whole USA's 1980s cocaine and crack boom. Once this operation went underground, Oliver North partnered with Noriega in Panama to train and support the Contras. Because of this, Noriega, an international drug dealer and arch-criminal, was paid well by the US.

But it wasn't just drug smuggling that was needed to fund the Contras; they also needed to launder their money. With the help of the CIA, it would not be a problem, as cutouts like a shrimp company are used to wash their dirty money. The CIA worked with criminal organizations like the Medellin cartel, in which it is said that future President and ex-CIA Director George Bush himself worked directly with Pablo Escobar.

Just like with LSD a few decades earlier, the US media operated in concert and collusion with the government to parrot anti-drug hysteria that was not based on data or reality in any way. Corporate media outlets like AP and the NYT called crack the nation's drug of choice and said there were waves of crack addicts destroying the fabric of America. This was, of course, based on zero supporting scientific evidence, in which the media only quotes and references law enforcement and anti-drug political advocates.

The CIA Contra drugs and arms smuggling operation was a complete loop and self-perpetuating system, just like the Golden Triangle was before it. The Contras, being sold to the American public by the Reagan administration as freedom fighters who would halt the horrors of Communism in Central America, along with the CIA, were responsible for the birth of the LA crack market and the massive influx of cocaine into the USA in the 1980s.

Contra cocaine and money are what allowed LA gangs like the Crips and Bloods to get so powerful, arming them with advanced weapons straight from CIA-connected arms dealers, giving the Reagan administration some nice villains to target their racist anti-drug propaganda against. That was used as justification to ramp up anti-crack and drug laws, further inciting more repression of the lower minority classes.

Meanwhile, all the upper-level drug dealers and smugglers were protected from up high by the CIA, which acted as a mafioso enforcer and the US-aligned drug dealers' best friend, protector, and compatriot. Well, for as long as they were of use to us.

As far as the local police, like the LAPD, go, they were more interested in profiting personally from their seizure of drug dealers' property and luxury goods, as they were accused of beatings, theft, property destruction, and false arrests.

The three books I primarily drew on for The Drug to Control are among the most important pieces of investigative journalism on illegal drugs ever published in the US. How strange that none of these authors, and none of their data, is ever used in any government communication of drugs and their implied drawbacks? The only information and data ever used by corporate media outlets are from anti-drug advocates in the police and government. They are people and institutions with an agenda, and that agenda is not to make you happy, healthy, and safe. Their agenda is to exercise power and implement control for those who direct them, the owner and ruling classes. In this, the drug war is an expression of the class war, in which lower classes and undesirables from the upper classes (dissidents) are vilified, criminalized, and imprisoned for supposed crimes that the upper crust is wholly insulated from.

Do not, at any time, expect to get authentic journalism on the drug war from the supposed pillars of American truth like the LA Times, New York Times, or The Washington Post. For decades, they have been parroting the company line, aka the government's and the owner class's line, and presenting it to the public as authentic oversight.

The end of this story is the fact that there is no end. There was and will continue to be no oversight of the CIA or its collaborators. They walked away from their crimes in the 50s, 60s, 70s, and 80s with little more than a public tongue-lashing from performative congressional committees.

The drug war as a method for generating revenue for illegal military operations continues to this day, all hidden under a cloak of mystery and top-secret designations. But one can only imagine how this is being leveraged in today's hotspots, from Ukraine to Gaza.

And the US government's mind control programs only moved more underground and overseas after congressional hearings in the 1970s. One can only guess how these programs have advanced and been implemented in varying degrees against the US public and its captured colonies over the past 50 years.

This is a book of common sense, and it is addressed to the inhabitants of America, every single one of them.